Communications Skills
for Project Managers

G. Michael Campbell

American Management Association

New York • Atlanta • Brussels • Chicago • Mexico City
San Francisco • Shanghai • Tokyo • Toronto • Washington, D.C.

This publication is designed to provide accurate and authoritative information in regard
to the subject matter covered. It is sold with the understanding that the publisher is not
engaged in rendering legal, accounting, or other professional service. If legal advice or
other expert assistance is required, the services of a competent professional person should
be sought.

"PMI" and the PMI logo are service and trademarks of the Project Management Institute,
Inc., which are registered in the United States of America and other nations; "PMP" and
the PMP logo are certification marks of the Project Management Institute, Inc., which are
registered in the United States of America and other nations; "PMBOK," "PM Network,"
and "PMI Today" are trademarks of the Project Management Institute, Inc., which are
registered in the United States of America and other nations; ". . . building professionalism
in project management . . ." is a trade and service mark of the Project Management
Institute, Inc., which is registered in the United States of America and other nations;
and the Project Management Journal logo is a trademark of the Project Management
Institute, Inc.

PMI did not participate in the development of this publication and has not reviewed the
content for accuracy. PMI does not endorse or otherwise sponsor this publication and
makes no warranty, guarantee, or representation, expressed or implied, as to its accuracy
or content. PMI does not have any financial interest in this publication, and has not
contributed any financial resources.

Library of Congress Cataloging-in-Publication Data

Campbell, G. Michael, 1948–
    Communications skills for project managers / G. Michael Campbell. --
1st ed.
        p. cm.
    Includes index.
    ISBN-13: 978-0-8144-1053-0
    ISBN-10: 0-8144-1053-7
    1. Project management.   2. Communication in management.   I. Title.

    HD69.P75C364 2009
    658.4'5--dc22   2008055732

Printing number
10 9 8 7 6 5 4 3 2 1

Contents

Acknowledgments

I would like to thank Bob Shuman for providing excellent guidance and suggestions. I have appreciated the opportunity to work with such a terrific editor and organization.

To Michael Snell, my agent, for presenting me with the chance to write a book that matches my passion so well. To Josh Pospisil for making the graphics look so professional.

To my wife, Molly, who continues to support my dreams. Her love and the love of my family remain the foundation of my life.

And to you, the readers, who have purchased this book. I understand how important projects are to your personal and professional success. I feel honored that you believe I can teach you a little something about communications in your quest to become a better project manager.

Introduction

Thinking About Your Project Communications in a New Way

Today, business is changing faster than ever, and most of those changes are being implemented through projects that require even stronger project management. Demand for project management methods and skills has driven the dramatic growth in organizations such as the Project Management Institute. However, just using sound project management methodology will not guarantee successful projects, as many project managers have learned to their dismay.

Why Isn't Good Project Management Enough?

Too many project managers have been in the situation where a project, which was a technical success from a project management perspective, was viewed as a business failure from the point of view of an operations group. How can that be possible—to be a "technical success" and "business failure"? In the Information Technology world where it frequently happens, it means the software application works as advertised and therefore is, by definition, a technical success. However, the user groups either don't use the application correctly, or they don't use it at all! As a result, the project never produces the projected business value—and is considered a business failure.

This book is designed to help you overcome that daunting hurdle and several others that are caused by the wrong communication strategy. I will show you in a step-by-step way how to use communications to deliver a successful business project and bring the business benefits promised.

Why Are Project Communications So Important?

As recently as twenty years ago, the only time you might come across the use of project management techniques was in the development of high-technology products at places like NASA or in engineering or heavy construction. Outside of the military, aerospace, defense, electronics, and building industries, project management tools and techniques were rarely used, and then only portions of those available were put into action. Even in companies and organizations where project management methodology was well established, the focus on communications was minimal. Usually, these companies were building large capital projects where people could often see and mark progress. Also, people had different expectations—when they moved into a new building or plant, they fully expected things to be different—and better! In today's era where more and more projects are centered on information, progress and other factors are not so clear. And the expectations are different. People expect the project to allow them to do the same work, only faster and easier. Managing expectations is a key driver for effective project communications.

Another piece of data about the importance of communications: My company, MCA International, was conducting a series of workshops for the project managers for an oilfield services company with locations literally all over the globe. In conducting these workshops, we worked with over 500 project managers representing over thirty countries. As part of the workshop evaluation, we asked these project managers to assess what made projects successful and what caused projects to fail. *The number one success factor* identified by this diverse group was communications. When we asked for more details, what we learned was that when communications were strong among the project team members and between the project team and the customers within the energy companies, the projects were nearly always successful. If the projects failed, poor communications was *always* identified as a critical factor in pinpointing what went wrong.

The other key success factor these project managers identified was the support and engagement of leadership in their projects. It seems that all project managers recognize the need for leadership backing, but are often frustrated in their efforts to get it. That is why the second chapter in this book, titled Preparing the Leadership, is right at the front of the book. It will demonstrate how you can keep the company leadership interested in your project from beginning to end. With vigorous project communications, your chances of success soar and your frustration will fall off dramatically.

What Happens If You Ignore Project Communications?

To illustrate the consequences of ignoring communications in managing expectations, I would like to relate the personal experience of one of my clients. His team was installing a new software application for traders who buy and sell commodities. He had used most of the communication techniques you will read in this book, and things had gone very well. However, my client found himself in the same tough situation that all project managers find themselves in at one time or another. It was a long project coming into the final months. However, because the project team began to get sloppy with its communications, the traders' expectations were not being managed carefully, and a storm of resistance to the new software began to build up. Unfortunately, if something wasn't done quickly, the final few months threatened to undo all the goodwill that had been built up over the previous 18 months within the commodities group. While many of the issues that caused the resistance were more complex than is necessary to detail here, the critical failure factor in this instance was a basic flaw in his communication strategy (the earlier reference to "sloppy"). The project manager and his team had fallen into the habit of communicating with the business users only through email. As most of us know, between the tremendous amount of daily email (most of it barely necessary) coupled with spam, most people will ignore email after a while, particularly if it is seen as simply "a status update." This is what happened to this project manager. So how did he fix the problem? First, the team worked together and, instead of relying on only email updates, he built a new and more hearty communications plan (see Chapter 10: Developing the Communications for the Project) that provided several "rich" communication events such as brown-bag lunches and town hall meetings (richness is explained in more details in Chapter 5: Common Elements for All Communications) in addition to email updates and personal phone calls. We also created a series of very targeted messages to key commodity traders who could influence others on their team. These changes, and some other technical fixes, helped him to finish the project with the amount of goodwill that the project team deserved based on the terrific job they had done.

So What Will You Get from This Book?

This book will give you the foundation of all communications, whether written or oral. Chapter 5: Common Elements for All Communications covers the basics for all types of communications and helps you build those communications for the maximum effect.

Throughout the book, you will see a wide variety of tools, templates, and techniques to help you prepare and deliver these communications for a wide range of audiences and purposes.

In Chapter 12: Using Communication to Handle Risks, you will see how effective communications can help you manage an assortment of risks. This is important because new technology has increased business risk and, consequently, the requirement for high degrees of project management competency in communications. It has raised the ante for project success due, in no small part, to the extraordinary investments companies have made by implementing new technologies and systems. Now the management teams of these organizations are demanding the same Return on Investment (ROI) that they would expect after building a refinery or any other major capital project.

A good illustration of the growing acceptance of project management methodology is the phenomenal growth of the Project Management Institute (PMI), the world's largest nonprofit professional organization that promotes the art and science of project management. Founded in 1969 with fewer than 100 members, by 1979 membership was still only 2,000. By 1990, the organization still had less than 10,000 members. However, by the turn of the century, membership had swollen to 50,000. As of the writing of this book, PMI boasts over 150,000 active members residing in 140 countries across the globe.

Business Project Management

The wide varieties of demands placed on organizations today quite naturally affect your individual approach to work. If you want to survive and thrive in these changing times, you must be effective in both your field of expertise (the ordinary work you do) as well as in your ability to rally with others to solve problems, pursue opportunities, and effect change (the project work). That requires competency in both project management and communications. Most people would have a tough time trying to figure out the link between project management and change management (*change management* is a structured approach to transitioning individuals, teams, and organizations from the status quo to a desired future state; the current definition of change management includes both change management processes and individual change management models, which together are used to manage the people side of changes) as disciplines. *Project management* is seen as more of a methodology with defined tasks, hard deliverables, and standard techniques. Change management, on the other hand, is seen as the "soft" side—the people side. Project managers who have thought about change management usually think about it as communications, including posters on the wall, and maybe some training. However, ask most project managers some pointed questions such as, "What is the most difficult part of your project?" and nearly all of them will respond, "People!" If you follow up with another question, "Why are people the hardest part?" they will usually respond, "Because they always resist the changes that my project requires."

If that is generally true, then maybe there is a link between project management and change management. But most project managers are probably like me: We think in processes, meaning we like a systematic set of steps to reach a predictable conclusion and, while we multitask, we do much better with methodologies such as the approach proposed by the Project Management Institute, or PRINCE2 developed by the Office of Government Commerce in the United Kingdom, than "flying by the seat of our pants." This linkage is called "Business Project Management."

So this book will show you how to link project management methods, as outlined by the Project Management Institute (PMI), with change management methods and how communications impacts each phase of a project. The book will follow the four phases of PMI's methodology and show you how to build them together at each phase.

Finally, throughout the book, you will find a series of reminders that will aid you as you work your projects in the future. They will allow you to recall the major points to consider without the effort of reading the book again or trying to figure out where those points are in each chapter. I believe that will allow you to replicate your success over and over again.

Case Study

During the course of the book, you will be referred to a case study. In this case study, the names have been changed to protect the participants, but the situations and solutions are real. The hope is that the case study will aid you in understanding how to apply the communication techniques that are recommended in this book and see how another project manager used them successfully. Our case study for the concepts in the book will be a company, MedTech Supply Company, that manufactures and services a broad line of healthcare products, such as hospital beds, bedding and linens, and specialty items for helping speed up the healing process, to hospitals, nursing homes, and doctors' offices. The company has had trouble growing its business over the past few years. As a publicly traded company, the management team has been under increasing pressure from Wall Street to improve both its profit margins and prospects for growth in the future. If it could not improve the prospects of the company quickly, its only option was to sell the company to a competitor (which would leave all of them looking for new jobs).

After conducting a series of strategy sessions to understand their strengths, weaknesses, opportunities, and threats (the traditional SWOT), it became apparent to the leadership team that the best chance of accelerating growth was to sell more products to existing customers. In order to accomplish that goal, leadership needed to do a better job of understanding the customer base. The Sales and Marketing people provided research indicating it cost twice as much to capture and service new customers as opposed to existing ones. They also determined sales territories and services lines were structured so that customers lacked information and the sales team had difficulty cross-selling (anyone who has been asked to buy an extended warranty after purchasing a television or other electronic device will recognize cross-selling techniques). After some deliberation on various options, the company's management decided it needed to capture customer information better using a customer relationship management (CRM) software application. This type of software should allow the company to accomplish its dual goals of better customer service combined with higher growth. They decided to name the project Project Renewal.

As we move through this case study during the course of the book, it will become evident that nearly everyone in the organization is touched in one way or another by this project, as well as MedTech's customers. That makes communications even more important because of the number of stakeholders, both internal and external (I will cover stakeholders in Chapter 5: Common Elements for All Communications). You will see the cast of characters who had a significant role during the project in Figure I.1. Of course there were many others, but these are the key players for this book.

Sponsor: Lisa Ramsay
Champion: Paula Dahlbert

Working Committee:
Leeland Olson, Controller
Carrie Jenkins, Customer Relations Manager
Chuck Swindle, Vendor Management and Contacts
Gary Stiles, Sales Manager
Walter Fisher, Manufacturing Manager
Dan Cohen, Director IT (as needed)

Project Team:
Rod Thompson, Project Manager
Anne Garcia, Communication Specialist and CM Leader
Paul Ryan, Lead Business Analyst
Joshua Larsen, Technical Team Lead
Luke Johnson, Liaison with IT

FIGURE I.1   MedTech Project Renewal cast.

The Payoff

Just think of how great it will feel when you make your final presentation to the steering committee after successfully completing your project. Imagine how much your peers will envy you because you have delivered such a great project and the customers were truly delighted with the results! And in your mind, you will know that you can do it again every time!

Here are some quotes from others who have tried these techniques:

> Now I understand the importance of good communication to a successful project—Project Manager, UK

> Anyone participating in projects should know these concepts!—Project Team Lead, Italy

> This made me realize that very good communication between all the members of the project team and the project management is key to success.—Project Team Lead, Venezuela

> In addition to good communication, having a realistic plan as a guide is what I learned most.—Project Manager, Houston, Texas

> After taking this course, I realized that the problems we've had in projects are the communications between different levels. First: Identifying the needs of the client and then communicating this necessity to your superior or other responsible people. Second: Communication between our team, because sometimes we do the same task again because we do not have good communication.—Project Team Lead, Mexico City

Chapter 1

Linking Projects and Strategy Through Effective Communications

All projects are generally undertaken because they are a part of the plan to take an organization to a new level of performance. Figure 1.1 demonstrates the idea. Every business must do two things at the same time to succeed: Run the business every day to meet targets and goals, and change the business so that it can grow and survive into the future. The "V" represents the vision the company has; the way it will fit into the competitive landscape of the future. Balancing these two demands is why projects are so very difficult.

One of the first communication challenges for the project manager is communicating how the project will make the company better when it is finished (the vision). Too often the executive team that sanctioned the project will only have a high-level, strategic vision that can be very difficult to communicate to the rank-and-file within the company. For people in the company to relate to the purpose of the project, they will need much more in the way of concrete examples. For example, the management team stated that the company wanted to be "number one in customer satisfaction in

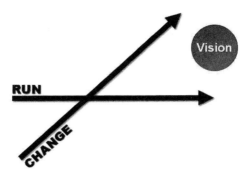

FIGURE 1.1   The dual nature of Run the Business while Changing the Business—and projects always are part of the Change the Business axis. The pressure to Run the Business will always supersede the Change the Business agenda. Source: *Change Is the Rule* by W. E. "Dutch" Holland, Dearborn Press. Reprinted with permission.

the hospital equipment business." However, that still didn't provide the project manager with very much to communicate to the company on the value of the project. The case for change discussed in Chapter 6: Writing the Case for Change will provide you with a template for asking management the right questions—and getting the right answers. In fact, after asking the right questions, Rod Thompson, the project manager, recognized that the new CRM system was needed to support a modern equipment manufacturing company. The old system was unreliable and would no longer be supported by the original vendor. So the improved customer satisfaction was really about being flexible and responsive to the needs of customers in the marketplace—that was really the vision he needed to get across.

The dynamics of communication become particularly difficult when companies are trying to do those "Change the Business" projects (like Rod's CRM project) with the same staff that must also do its "day jobs" and fit the project work in around it.

All businesses have activities on the "Run the Business" arrow that focus on their periodic results (usually, but not exclusively, financial)—monthly, quarterly, and yearly.

Every successful company has excellent processes and procedures for managing and controlling the activities on this arrow. Rod understood that the difficulty for line managers at MedTech is how their performance is measured. They were measured on their Run the Business activities. When their key players were drawn into project work, it jeopardized the ability to deliver results. That meant that in any conflicting priorities, the line managers would automatically default to an employee's Run the Business responsibilities.

Therefore, as project manager, Rod had to communicate regularly with the supervisors of the people who were on his project team. The messages to these managers were structured and composed to convince them that there are benefits to them, as well as the company, in allowing their key people to participate in the project. Rod gave them regular updates on the contribution of their direct reports about every two weeks so the value these people were bringing to the project was clearly evident.

Therefore, management was creating high-stakes initiatives (usually broken down into projects) that will change the business in the future and position the company effectively for the long term. Progress along both of these two paths—simultaneously—is necessary for survival. Project Renewal was just such a project for MedTech.

As we all know, without changing over time, any business will end up like the buggy whip industry—gone! Rod knew it was important to remember this dual focus concept as a cornerstone to all the communications he initiated. Ultimately, he made sure that all project communications had a common root in the linkage of the initiative to the broader business strategy outlined by the executive team.

In our case study, the MedTech leadership decided to ensure that they had equal focus on both agendas and divided their weekly management meeting on Mondays. In the morning they would work on Run the Business activities, and after lunch the focus would shift to Change the Business projects such as Project Renewal. If you do not see a similar commitment to focusing on Change the

Business projects in companies, it should be a red flag for you as the project manager. It indicates that the level of executive commitment to sustain support over the long haul could be difficult to sustain. And this is really the way the executive team communicates to the project team and stakeholders regarding its commitment and expectations for tangible results.

Projects to Change the Business

There is an interesting statistic provided by over 80 executives in a recent survey. They concluded that only 40 percent of their employees would change their working habits and adopt the project deliverables coming from their high-tech projects. That is a disturbing statistic if we remember that these companies are using these same projects as the vehicle for executing the Change the Business agenda. Those change projects may take many different forms. For example, they may be projects around technology implementations that we found in the survey, but they may also include

- Strategy initiatives
- Information technology or systems
- Business development initiatives
- Human resource performance

Figure 1.2 illustrates the process: Any and all of these projects usually start with a decision about what the customers will require from the company in the future; these initiatives are usually focused on meeting or exceeding these customer requirements or needs. The requirements are then put into a strategic plan that will be carried out over the period of anywhere from a few months to as many as five years. In addition, these requirements are converted into various projects for execution. Finally, all of these initiatives must be eventually migrated into the organization as part of the day-to-day business so that the changes they prompt become part of the Run the Business operations. These projects may have a variety of outcomes in the forecast, but one constant remains—the need to improve per-

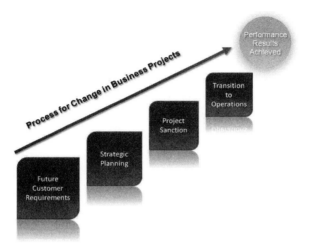

FIGURE 1.2   All projects are undertaken to improve the performance of the business, and they all follow roughly this path of understanding the future requirements of the customer, completing the strategic plan to address those future requirements, sanctioning projects to implement the strategic plan, and then transitioning from the project to ongoing operations.

formance in the future. Project managers must understand this link. The project manager must also communicate and make sure that each member of the project team understands the link to the future of the organization and the performance results the business is trying to achieve. Why, you may ask? The answer is relatively simple as a concept, but much harder to execute. That was precisely the situation with MedTech. They were facing tough competition, and they were finding that their old, reliable business of beds, bedding, and various supplies was simply not growing. Wall Street (and MedTech's investors) were looking for the executive team to provide direction on the growth in the future. Using Project Renewal and the customer relationship management (CRM) system to expand sales was a key to convincing Wall Street MedTech had a future.

As the project proceeded, the project manager, Rod Thompson, and the project team were required to make numerous decisions to overcome a wide variety of technical and business problems that were unforeseen at the start. If you have participated on a project team in the past, you may have experienced something similar. There is rarely only one way to address a particular business issue or technical problem. At MedTech, Rod Thompson realized that if he and the key project team members did not have an understanding of how the executive team envisioned the strategy for using the CRM to build the future business, the project team might have made decisions that would not allow the finished project to achieve the business results. These results were what the MedTech executives intended when they originally authorized the project. It comes back to the concept that Stephen Covey (borrowed from St. Augustine) described in his book *Seven Habits of Successful People*, "start with the end in mind."

The MedTech executives decided to make Lise Ramsay, Vice President, Marketing, the project sponsor. She would be held responsible for delivering the business value of Project Renewal. To stay abreast of the developments in the project, she would report to them every Monday afternoon at their leadership team meeting for Change the Business projects. In addition, once a month they invited project manager Rod Thompson to attend the leadership team meeting and update the entire team on the status of Project Renewal.

Start with the Expected Business Benefits

Rod realized right from the start that he would need to align the project with the business needs and requirements since it was the only reason MedTech undertook the project in the first place! He recognized that he must start with the expected business benefits. Most important, benefits should include the anticipated savings or revenue increases that would occur once the project is completed.

Companies format their business case templates in many ways, but MedTech's format included these items:

- Business reasons the company undertook the project—typically the problem the project is trying to solve or the increase in performance it is trying to achieve.

- Options that were considered in addressing the problem or performance requirements (since there is rarely one way to address the issue).
- Tangible benefits that the company hoped to achieve as the result of Project Renewal becoming a successful project. (Later in the chapter, you will see that these benefits need to be clearly measurable and feasible.)
- Brief analysis of the high-level risks. (There will be a much more in-depth discussion about communicating risks in Chapter 12: Using Communications to Handle Risks.)

A brief overview of the costs to establish the budget and a schedule with key milestone dates provided were also part of the business case. All of these are important because Rod will have to communicate this information multiple times during the course of the project. He recognized that people will forget over time if they are not reminded. And he needed to make sure he communicated all these key ideas to the members of his project team.

The business case for most projects will include a cost/benefit analysis. As a rule, if a project depends on only one key benefit to justify it, it is very risky. Why? Because most projects have several benefits, so if one is not achieved, others still make the project worthwhile. Rod took the course that most companies and project managers take: He worked from the assumption that MedTech would not change anything (e.g., no customer relationship system and no attempts to improve cross-selling to existing customers) and then worked through the potential options referred to earlier for solving the problem.

Conducting a Feasibility Study

The executives at MedTech asked Rod, as the project manager, and key team members to conduct a *feasibility study* to see if the project made sense from an economic

> **Definition**
> A *feasibility study* is a general estimate used to make a decision about whether to pursue a particular project.

or business point of view. The purpose of the study was to identify any make-or-break issues that might prevent the project from being successful: in other words, to decide whether the project made good business sense. The information developed in the feasibility study provided good input into the building of the data related to the business benefits.

Developing a Feasibility Study for Project Renewal

For MedTech's Project Renewal, Rod Thompson needed to be able to answer some very specific questions:

1. How do we know that our customers will buy more of our products if we offer them? Will we be able to capture the right information to answer that question?
2. Why do we believe that we have the capability to deliver Project Renewal? Is the CRM technology the right solution or is some other solution more appropriate?
3. Will you, as project manager, be able to manage the risks associated with this type of project? What are risks you have identified so far?
4. How much do you estimate it will cost to develop the CRM solution for Project Renewal (including license fees, cost of ownership, data analysis, etc.), and what is the payback period? What kind of return will MedTech see with this investment?

Rod knew that examples abound of companies that initiated major projects and then flushed millions of dollars down the drain because they didn't conduct a

Words for the Wise

The project should be stopped if the viability of the business benefits disappears for any reason. For example, if the assumptions made at MedTech about the cost and time required to implement the CRM had been wrong and it would have actually taken three times as much money and time, MedTech might have made the decision to immediately halt the project.

proper feasibility study. Consider Dell Computer, the large computer manufacturer, and its Enterprise Resource Planning (ERP) software program, which promised to provide instant access to all the information managers needed to run their business. They tried and tried to make the system work to their customized requirements. Finally, they gave up and abandoned a project in which they had more than $50 million invested!

Rod wanted to avoid similar mistakes, so he knew he needed to clearly define some points before the management team committed to the project:

- Goals that identify the need for the project and the measurable benefits expected by the stakeholders and users.
- Clearly defined scope.
- Commitment of the time needed to complete the project by the business stakeholders, particularly the leadership team.
- Rough estimate of timeline, resource requirements, and costs.

Doing this work up front gave Rod's project more credibility and manageability.

Clear Project Goals Make Sense to Everyone

The Dell story illustrates an important concept about setting appropriate goals for your projects: Set realistic goals or you probably will not be able to reach them. Here is additional advice regarding setting project goals:

- Any project you undertake must make sense in terms of an overall goal that benefits people in some way. If a project doesn't have a benefit for someone, why bother? Another way to look at this is to make sure the project goals specify how completing the project will make things better than they would be without the project. You should be able to clearly describe the outcomes and benefits to stakeholders and end users.

- Carefully think out project goals; consider even the most obvious questions to make sure the idea is really as good as people think it is.
- Project goals should provide the criteria you need to evaluate the success in completing a project. These criteria include measures of the time, costs, and resources required to achieve desired outcomes.

> It concerns us to know the purpose we seek in life, for then, like archers aiming at a definite mark, we shall be more likely to attain what we want.
>
> *Aristotle*

- Review project goals with the core team and reach consensus before moving into the next phase of the project.

Of course, you can use project management techniques on enterprises with inappropriate goals and still accomplish something, but you may fail to do anything useful. For example, one of the biggest complaints about Information Technology (IT) projects is that end users perceive them as a waste of time. Often, the IT department is totally baffled by such claims. In a software application project (as a typical example), IT people point out, usually quite correctly, that the software works just as advertised. The problem often centers on the fact that people don't know how to use the software to get their jobs done, or they remain unconvinced that the software makes things better. As a result, the software rapidly becomes "shelfware" because it never gets off the shelf. Was the project a success? Maybe from a technical point of view, you could argue that it was if the application runs as specified. However, from a practical point of view, it was a failure. If your key customers don't like the product you have produced for them, then the project is a failure regardless of whether it technically works.

The Primary Goals of Every Project

Every project has three primary goals:

1. To create something (such as a product, procedure, organization, building, or other deliverable).

2. To complete it within a specific budgetary framework.
3. To finish it within an agreed-upon schedule.

Beyond these goals are other goals that must be specified and that actually define the project. For example, it's not enough to have the goal of building a mid-priced sports car. A more appropriate set of goals would be to build a mid-priced, convertible sports car that will:

- Use both gas and electric power.
- Be of a quality comparable to the Volvo C70.
- Sell for 10 percent less than all comparable cars.
- Offer specific features to meet competitive demand, such as antilock brakes, a geonavigational system, onboard Internet access, and an electrically powered convertible top.
- Be available for the 2010 sales year.
- Be manufactured by the factory in the United States but designed by the engineers in Japan.

The bullet points above might be described as requirements. Requirements are those conditions or attributes that a project must meet to satisfy the contract or other agreements such as the project charter.

Risk Management

Taking over someone else's goals can be difficult. If you aren't in on the goal-setting process, carefully review what is expected before you assume the project. Make sure the goals are complete and well-formed. If they are off base, ask to review and revise them with the sponsor or other key stakeholders. If you're not given that opportunity, consider looking elsewhere. It's better to decline the offer than to be responsible for an ill-defined project that you can be blamed for later.

MedTech's goals for Project Renewal were defined as the installation of a usable customer relationship management system to

- Capture all customer profile information (e.g., addresses, locations, key personnel) accurately.
- Create reports that will allow the management team and the marketing team to analyze each customer's
  - History of purchases and whether incentive discounts affected buying patterns.
  - Future buying trends as an input to Marketing and the Research and Development group as predictors for future product development.
  - Credit limits and purchasing trends related to those limits.
- Allow the easy retrieval of all contracts with terms and conditions related to each customer's purchases.

The executive team decided that attempting to load all the historical data from the old legacy systems would be out of scope for Project Renewal. They made the decision that trying to re-create the past would be too expensive for the potential value it might bring.

Having this kind of guidance from the management team about scope, feasibility, and the benefits they are looking for was critical to the success of Project Renewal. However, many project managers struggle to receive that kind of support.

Key Points to Remember

- All projects create changes in the way business operates.
- Always focus communications on the expected benefits.
- A feasibility study is really all about answering four specific questions about the project.
- Make sure the goals are well-defined and management has ratified them.

In the next chapter, let's look at how Rod Thompson used communications to obtain the kind of management engagement he needed to succeed.

Chapter 2

Preparing the Leadership

In the last chapter, we saw the guidance Rod Thompson received as he started Project Renewal—he had goals, defined benefits, and a clear definition of the scope.

The Project Management Institute has done several studies on the critical success factors involved in executing a successful project. Nearly all of them have concluded that management leadership and support are critical. Why? Because people respond to the agenda their "boss" feels is important. And how do they determine what is important to their boss? They read the signals: Notice what the boss talks about and pays attention to on a day-to-day basis. If you consider your own situation, you probably use this primary technique as well.

How Involved Should the Leadership Be?

While the leadership will seldom have the time to be in on the details concerning the activities and tasks, it will be important for the project manager to communicate specific roles and responsibilities for them. The project manager must communicate to the leadership team that at certain times during the project, he or she will call upon them to participate actively and deliver particular messages or intervene when difficulties occur. For example, if you need a leader to give an important message to the organization about expecting commitment from people for the project, he or she should be willing to do that.

Here is one example at MedTech: One area that required a message from the CEO concerned the leadership team's commitment to Project Renewal and that they expected the same commitment from all of employees. The CEO had to let people know that the project was important to him personally. Of course, a similar message could have come from Lise Ramsay as the sponsor. But Ms. Ramsay was the Vice President of Marketing. Who would have really paid attention to that message? Probably only the Marketing Department! However, everyone in MedTech is ultimately responsible to the CEO. That is why he has to deliver the message. In our case study, Rod Thompson (the Project Renewal project manager) and Anne Garcia (the Communications and Change Management Lead) carefully crafted the initial announcement regarding Project Renewal. Then they presented the draft to Lise Ramsay and worked with her to edit it. Their goal in working with Lise was to make it sound more like the words the organization would understand while, at the same time, being careful to maintain the foundation of the message. This was the model they followed for all the communications coming from the members of the executive team throughout the project.

Once Rod, Anne, and Lise finished editing the message, they submitted it for review. In MedTech, protocol dictated that all communications coming from the CEO must be screened by the corporate communications people. Unfortunately, much of the material developed by corporate communications had a much different purpose than what Project Renewal needed. As a result, Rod and Anne had to do some work convincing this group that a press-release style would not convey the message they needed. By reviewing the purpose and the power base concepts (discussed in Chapter 5: Common Elements for All Communications), they prevailed. The CEO did approve the draft with few revisions and sent the message about Project Renewal.

Here is how the message went out:

To: All employees

From: Donald Dearborn

I am pleased to announce that we have made the decision to implement a Customer Relationship Management (CRM) system within MedTech. We are looking for a usable system that will allow us to capture all customer profile information (e.g., addresses, locations, key personnel, and other information) accurately and generate reports that will allow the management team and the marketing team to analyze each customer's history of purchases and whether incentive discounts affected buying patterns. We also want to use the system to understand future buying trends as an input to Marketing and the Research and Development group as predictors for future product development.

In these difficult economic times, we also need quick access to customer credit limits and purchasing trends related to those limits with easy retrieval of all contracts, including terms and conditions related to each customer's purchases.

On behalf of the leadership team at MedTech, I want to emphasize our support for Project Renewal and express my appreciation to members of the Working Committee [you will learn more about this group later in the chapter] and the project team for the support they have shown so far.

Finally, I would appreciate your support for the project. There will be further communications following this announcement providing you with greater detail as we move toward implementation.

As you can see from this message, this was one of those times and messages that must come from the leadership team to have the impact and credibility required to achieve the desired support.

Therefore, the project manager must develop a detailed communications plan (see Chapter 10: Developing the Communications for the Project) that highlights to the leadership when they will be called on to send certain messages and that they are key people involved in the communications planning. Leaders are often more than willing to communicate to the organization if they understand how they can contribute and why it is important for the message to come from them personally.

However, use the same strategy that Rod did. If you are a strong communicator, this will usually mean that you, or someone from the project team if you are not a strong communicator, will be required to craft the message, or at least provide a draft, that the executive can deliver.

Risk Management

In most cases a company leader will want to review and edit the message so that it sounds more like the way he or she would deliver it. There's nothing wrong with that, as long as the basic idea stays intact. If the leader (or corporate communications) begins to edit the announcement in such a way that it loses the core meaning, you may need to do a better job of explaining what you are trying to accomplish and educate him or her on the risks and possible consequences involved in straying from the way you've developed the content.

If there is a communication specialist within the project team to develop the messages, you may need to get this person involved in the conversation. The specialist may have a better chance of explaining the intent of the wording and approach drafted, especially if he or she drafted it.

Also, many project managers deal with multiple layers of management during the course of planning and executing their projects. Mid-level managers in MedTech were notoriously difficult to deal with in times of change. And Project Renewal would be no different. The reason for the difficulty was fairly classic—they are the people who supervise most of the work done in the company. Remember the two arrows in the previous chapter about Run the Business and

Change the Business? These managers are focused only on Run the Business, and Project Renewal is from Change the Business agenda. If they do not understand or see visible evidence of commitment from the senior managers, they feel that their compliance is optional, not mandatory. Navigating these types of political waters required the help of the senior executives at times within MedTech. Occasionally, some of these mid-level managers challenged the project, probably as much to see the commitment of the executive team as to question some of the business decisions being made. It is beyond the pale of any project manager to address a challenge from this group.

In one example during the project, an issue arose about how Project Renewal should handle a customer's request for special orders. The managers in the sales department wanted the order filled quickly and efficiently to meet the customer's need and hoped to build goodwill by showing excellent responsiveness to the requests. However, the managers in the warehouse and shipping departments insisted the right paperwork be completed within the existing policies before they would authorize and ship any order. Clearly, the project team needed this conflict resolved. As Rod and Paula Dahlberg, the champion (you will learn more about the champion later in the chapter), explained to the leadership team, the project team could deliver either solution, but the team needed their help to know which way to go. This kind of decision was inappropriate for the project team to make without direction. The leadership team needed to help the project team resolve this type of situation. As might be expected, the leadership team came down on the side of sales. They directed the project team to work with sales, warehouse, and shipping to develop an expedited process for these situations, but the clear message was that paperwork was not to get in the way of a customer purchase.

Providing the Leadership with a Script

Although it is imperative that leadership become involved in a successful project, this is not always easy. BlessingWhite, the management consulting firm, reports that nearly half of the executives

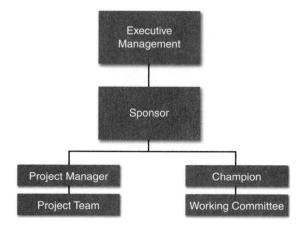

FIGURE 2.1   Simple governance model. This model shows that the Project Team and the Working Committee have separate roles, but they are both accountable to the Sponsor.

surveyed by them rated leading teams through organizational changes as extremely difficult or very challenging.[1] My firm, MCA International, determined that one of the best ways to lead these project changes was to identify key individuals for critical roles in the project. Figure 2.1 shows the relationship of these entities.

1. Sponsor: Ultimate authority with responsibility and accountability for the success of the project with responsibility for communicating with the executive leadership about Project Renewal.
2. Champion: Responsible for ensuring the business value of Project Renewal is realized within MedTech with responsibility for communicating with the business about Project Renewal.
3. Working Committee: People from the commercial parts of the company who will be responsible for delivering the business benefits of the project.

The idea of an executive sponsor has been around for a long time. I will not provide a lot of details on that role here because it

---

[1]*Consultant News*, August 17, 2007.

has been covered very well in other books, as well as the *Project Management Book of Knowledge* (PMBOK). However, as most of us who have managed projects for any length of time recognize, it is often very difficult to keep a sponsor engaged throughout a long project so he or she is ready to help you at key junctures in the project. That is why we turned to the additional role of project champion. The best candidate for champion has some critical characteristics to make a project successful:

- First and foremost, he or she is trusted explicitly by the sponsor and is able to provide that executive with clear and unambiguous information about the project, also delivering good news or bad news as well as requests for help.
- Second, he or she has a broad understanding that cuts across the various segments of the business that are impacted by the changes that the project will bring. Our most successful champions are usually people at the director level who have handled operational assignments in various parts of the organization.
- He or she acts as the chair of the working committee and leads that group.
- He or she works with the sponsor on cross-functional issues—for example, the steps in the approval process when the sales department wanted to extend the credit limit of a particular customer, but the credit department was clearly leaning in a different direction. Each of those departments has different bosses, and someone was going to have to navigate the issues and come to a resolution.

Paula Dahlberg, Director of Marketing and Customer Service, fits all those criteria within MedTech. She was chosen by Lise Ramsay to fill the role as the champion.

Meet the Key Players

Sponsor–Lise Ramsay, Vice President, Marketing

Champion–Paula Dahlberg, Director, Marketing and Customer Service

The project sponsor's role includes the following:

1. Has the ultimate authority, responsibility, and accountability for the success of the project.
2. Provides support and direction to the project.
    2.1. Approves project Business Case.
    2.2. Approves the project plan and statement of work to maintain alignment with the overall objectives of the company.
    2.3. Assists in developoing project policies and procedures.
    2.4. Approves project deliverables.
    2.5. Approves changes to project scope and provides additional funds for changes as required.
3. Monitors the progress of the project.
    3.1. Continually monitors the project budget and schedule.
    3.2. Manages communications with senior management on the progress of the project.
    3.3. Escalates issues appropriate to the senior management for timely decisions.
4. Works with the champion.
    4.1. Makes business decisions for the project.
    4.2. Provides required resources to the project as needed.
    4.3. Shields the project from corporate politics.
    4.4 Works to resolve conflicts.

The project champion's role includes the following:

1. Is ultimately responsible for ensuring the business value for Project Renewal within the asset.
    1.1. Works with the asset project manager to understand the types of changes required for success within the company.
        1.1.1. Assesses the impact of various options prior to a decision.
        1.1.2. Acts as the approving authority for overall process design within the asset.

1.2. Identifies project risks and mitigation strategies for the company in cooperation with the Subject Matter Experts (SME) within the company.

1.3. Maintains the involvement of the project sponsor as appropriate.

    1.3.1 Assumes the responsibility of escalating issues that require the project sponsor to act or intervene.

    1.3.2 Actively communicates risks and mitigation strategies to the project sponsor as appropriate.

1.4. Coordinates and approves the content of the training for the CRM.

    1.4.1 Approves the content for the training prepared by the project manager.

    1.4.2 Coordinates the availability of personnel to attend training.

1.5. Is able to demonstrate the busines value of the project.

    1.5.1. Assists the project manager in developing performance measures and metrics to track and demonstrate business value realization.

    1.5.2. Takes ownership of the performance measurement system and metrics at the conclusion of the project.

2. Provides the focal point for two-way communication between the project team and the company.

    2.1. Serves as the key business communicator for the project.

        2.1.1. Stays current and communicates key project information.

        2.1.2. Understands the project status, issues, and next steps.

    2.2. Identifies the other influence leaders within the company and regularly consults with them to test ideas.

    2.3. Works cross-functional issues within the company.

    2.4. Puts major effort into "selling" the project.

        2.4.1. Promotes the benefits of CRM data to the company.

        2.4.2. Captures "success stories" for sharing within and without the company.

2.5. Informs the company of key changes affecting the project as they become apparent.

2.6. Translates those key changes for individuals to ensure that they understand and recognize the impacts or benefits.

2.6.1. Identifies "stragglers," i.e., those who are resisting the required changes and understands why they are resisting.

2.6.2. Is aware of, and reports on, any other factors within the company that impact the project.

2.7. Attends and actively participates in project meetings.

As you can see from the descriptions, one key role for the sponsor and champion is as communicators. Indeed, as a project manager, Rod Thompson drafted most of the communications such as emails, announcements, and presentations they made to the organization. However, it was very important that these critical communications came from them and not Rod. When we look at the stakeholder analysis in Chapter 5 (stakeholders are defined by the Project Management Institute as anyone who has a vested interest in the success of the project), one of the key questions will be who should deliver the message. In most cases of communication outside the project team, the communication should be delivered by either the sponsor or the champion—but more about that later.

After securing the champion, Lise and Rod helped Paula determine who should be part of the Working Committee team. In order to assist everyone in communicating who would participate in the project, Rod developed an organization chart (Figure 2.2) and published it under Lise's signature.

Developing a Working Committee and Working Groups

Rod Thompson, the successful project manager, believed these people were a critical extension of his project team. First of all, he conducted a stakeholder analysis of key people affected by the results

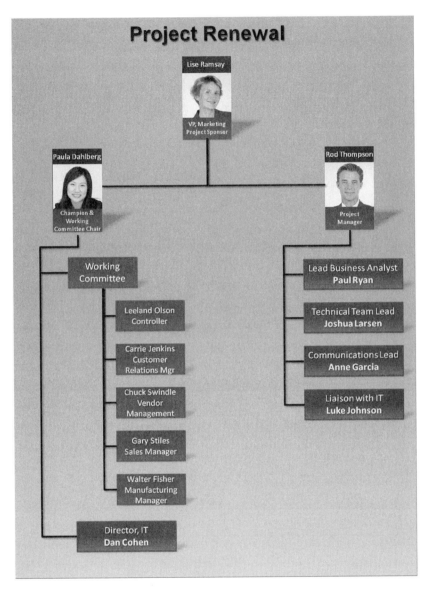

FIGURE 2.2   Project Renewal organization chart.

of the project. There are several considerations in pulling together a Working Committee and various working groups. As stated earlier, Rod worked with Lise and Paula (sponsor and champion) to identify and nominate the best key people the company had to offer.

Unfortunately, these same people were often asked to take on these types of roles because they are outstanding and respected. Rod explained to Lise and Paula that one key indication of lack of leadership support would be the unwillingness of leadership to provide these people for work on Project Renewal. This is a very risky strategy. Rod was determined that he would not be lured into taking people because they are "available" because there is usually a reason no one wants them working on his or her projects.

> The greatest difference between a working committee and a working group is that the Working Committee should remain intact throughout the project, whereas a working group is given a specific issue or problem to solve and then disbanded.

It was very important to pull in various departments or groups that were impacted by the changes the project would force on them when it was finished. The basic mandate for the Working Committee would be to consider various options that have been presented from the project team and make decisions about which option should be implemented

So, in our Project Renewal case study, we can see that nearly every department was affected by the project. Therefore, the project manager identified key players from sales, marketing, Information Technology, accounting, manufacturing, and procurement. In effect, these people represented a "constituency" within the company, and they needed to be aware of that role as part of Rod Thompson's orientation with them as he kicked off the Working

---

Risk Management

Working Committee for Project Renewal:

Controller:	Leeland Olson
Customer Relations Manager:	Carrie Jenkins
Vendor Management and Contracts:	Chuck Swindle
Sales Manager:	Gary Stiles
Manufacturing Manager:	Walter Fisher
Director IT:	Dan Cohen (as needed)

Committee. As the project team explores ways to implement the CRM solution named Project Renewal, the team was told to involve these key constituents routinely in the discussions about changes affecting the business.

Communications and the Working Committee

One of the key questions some of the members of the Working Committee had was "Why does this group have a role in communications during a project?" And that was a good question. Here was the answer. They are the vehicle—the eyes, ears, and voice—for keeping people informed about what the project was doing because they were going to be asked to follow a process for decision making that involves their constituency (the process will be detailed in Chapter 7). During Project Renewal at MedTech, Rod asked for and received agreement from the Working Committee members that before any key decision was made related to changes the project might make, the project manager would ask the Working Committee to conduct discussions with their constituency and poll them on their thoughts and concerns. This information was to be brought back to the project team for discussion before a decision was made.

Risk Management

Be aware that some Working Committee members will *not* discuss or inform their constituents and will attempt to make the decisions on their own. That really defeats the purpose of a Working Committee. To prevent this within Project Renewal, Rod Thompson developed independent relationships with other people within the various constituencies. He regularly sought them out to test what they were hearing from their Working Committee member and how knowledgeable they were about the project. That worked well for him, and he was able to specifically address any Working Committee members who were not communicating well with his concerns and include specific examples.

All these concerns could then be addressed, and the team could base its decision on the best way to get the job done for the business, not the slickest technical solution. This process helped keep Rod's project aligned with the business and commercial side. And if the business climate or landscape changed during the course of the project, the Working Committee would know and could provide the project team with fair warning.

The beauty of this arrangement is that the Working Committee was spreading the news about what was going on in the project. And after decisions were made, the Working Committee members were in a position to defend a decision later on if any constituency objected to any of the decisions. Ultimately, the most effective communication vehicle for serious messages came from people within the Working Committee that those groups impacted by the project both trusted and believed were looking out for their interests.

Communications and a Working Group

Working groups are often a subset of the Working Committee, but usually will also include other members with specific knowledge or expertise. Figure 2.3 shows a graphic configuration of working groups. Working groups will typically handle two types of issues where the problem is one that

1. Only affects a small group.
2. Uncovers a bad business practice that is outside the scope of the project.

Let's take a look at each of these situations, using MedTech's Project Renewal to illustrate the point.

As one example of issue 1, the project team ran into a conflict between the sales department and the accounting and invoicing departments. The issue was the relative importance of accurate information that must be entered into the CRM. The position of the

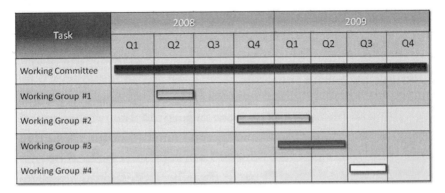

FIGURE 2.3   As you can see from the Gantt chart, the Working Committee is in place throughout the project. The working groups disband once their assignments are finished.

sales department is that they want to spend their time driving sales and identifying potential sales opportunities. They do not want to enter data into a computer. They see such tasks as relatively unimportant even as they recognize that accurate information could help them identify additional opportunities. On the other side of the equation is the accounting and invoicing group who must have accurate data and information to complete the company's financial reporting, not to mention receiving timely payment from customers. They complain that under the old way, they spent entirely too much time correcting input errors and conducting reconciliations.

In a situation like this one, other members of the Working Committee do not need to be involved in all the detailed aspects of this discussion, so Rod, the project manager, created a Working Group that included the representatives from sales and accounting as well as four other key individuals. This group was charged with exploring the options and coming back to the full Working Committee with two recommendations on

- The minimum information required for the end-to-end process to be effective, and
- Who would do the data entry into the CRM and why.

The project manager also requested the supporting rationale for the two recommendations. It was a way to get Working Group members to think through how they would explain the decisions (coincidentally, the project manager had the content for the communications surrounding the decision!).

You can begin to see the value of this approach for communicating project decisions related to data entry. Later on, if the accounting people grumbled about the lack of information or the sales team complained about entering orders into the CRM system, they could be reminded that their peers made the decision. It was endorsed by the full Working Committee and sanctioned by the senior management. That was a powerful message, delivered by the right people who have credibility with each group.

Second, projects often uncover bad business practices that are really out of the scope of the project. As an example in our Project Renewal case study, the project team learned that one of the key problems in moving contracts from sales to manufacturing for order scheduling was the length of time the legal department took reviewing contracts. It was pretty clear that Project Renewal should not take on a potential process problem within the legal department. Therefore, the project manager went to the champion and encouraged the organization of a working group consisting of sales, legal, and manufacturing to deal with this issue. This action meant that the issue was immediately taken out of the Working Committee's and the project team's scope of work. The champion was now responsible for getting that piece of work completed. Another major benefit is solving a serious business problem that was affecting customer responsiveness.

In both of these situations, the Working Committee and the working groups are acting as the primary communication vehicle related to the problems the project was seeking to solve, as well as the decisions that were being made. That is not to say that direct communications informing key stakeholders is no longer needed—any project manager must still do the job of ensuring that multiple communications continue. However, the job of communications is made much easier by using this approach.

Finally, you must realize that the biggest potential obstacle to the successful implementation of project deliverables is the middle management layer within the company. If you think about it, it makes perfect sense—middle managers are critical linchpins in the organization. You must keep these managers well informed so you are informed and aware of possible concerns they have regarding your project. Working Committee members can be the perfect people to communicate with these managers. If the project manager in Project Renewal was hearing concerns about the project from some of the manufacturing supervisors, who better to go with you to talk with them than the manufacturing representative from the Working Committee? We'll talk more about how to work with them and how to craft the messages when we get to the communications plan in Chapter 5. And in Chapter 11 we will see how to use the communication plan to address potential project risks.

Key Points to Remember

- Determine how involved the management needs to be in your project.
- Provide the appropriate leaders with a script on when you will call on them.
- Develop a Working Committee to make the business decisions related to the project.
- Identify a champion who can lead the Working Committee and also has the credibility to engage the leadership when their presence is required.

But first, every project manager much make sure he or she is working on the right project! That requires a very clear Project Charter and Statement of Work. The next chapter will demonstrate how to write these as a communication document as well as an artifact.

Chapter 3

Writing the Project Charter

The Project Management Institute's *Project Management Body of Knowledge* (PMBOK) identifies several key inputs into the project charter such as the problem the project is seeking to solve and the contract requirements the project must fulfill to be successful.[1] One of our firm's areas of expertise is in helping to recover projects that have gone wrong and to help put them back on track to deliver value. Almost without exception during our analysis of what went wrong, we uncover confusion on what the project was supposed to deliver—usually a misunderstanding between the project manager and one or more key stakeholders for the project. One of the keys to preventing that from happening is by using the project charter as a communications document with the key stakeholders, particularly the sponsor—the one who will supply the money and be accountable for the business results. As experienced project

---

[1] *Project Management Body of Knowledge* (Newton Square, PA: Project Management Institute, 2003), section 4.1.1.

managers know, the charter is the formal document that author-izes the project to move forward and the company to spend time and money on it. Many times the charter is developed, put on the shelf, and never referred to again. Near the end of the chapter, you will be able to read the charter that Rod Thompson wrote for Proj-ect Renewal. The most important part of the document is how he developed the content that went into it—and how he used the process as a communication vehicle for his project.

The charter provides a description of the work that is written in normal language. In the final section of this chapter, you will re-ceive some tips for writing the charter in a way that makes it a com-munication tool for you. Rod Thompson found using the charter a good way to discuss with key stakeholders the business outcomes for the project. As we saw earlier in the chapter, it became a great tool for working with the champion, Paula Dahlberg, and the spon-sor, Lise Ramsay, to clarify the business problem being solved by the project. Figure 3.3 is the Project Charter for Project Renewal. Tips for how to write the charter begin on page 40.

Let's focus on the following elements in the classic project charter (Figure 3.1) and determine how they are useful in develop-ing communications with your key stakeholders:

- Contract.
- Statement of the business problem that the project seeks to solve.
- Primary goals and objectives of the initiative.
- Project scope—including what the project will include and what it will *not* include.
- Assumptions and constraints that the project manager has determined.
- Benefits and risks in the early evaluations.
- Project budget and schedule.

If you are working on a project for someone outside your own company, you may have a draft of the charter as part of the con-

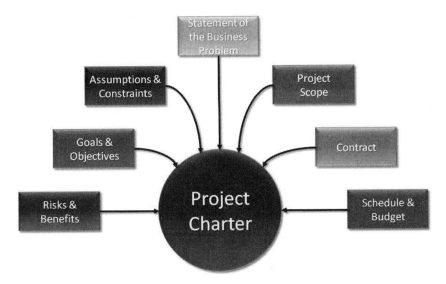

FIGURE 3.1   Inputs into the project charter include all of these important pieces of information.

tract. In other cases, the request for the initiative might come from an internal source, but there is an implicit contract in the ways the different parties should operate, so let us start with the contract.

Contract

A document of agreement (if there is one associated with your project) is obviously one of the first documents any project manager should review prior to starting any planning. The contract will specify the requirements and conditions that must be fulfilled if delivering a project to a customer outside the company. However, contracts are usually of limited use for helping a project manager communicate goals and objectives because they are written by attorneys and for attorneys. That is not a criticism, it is a fact. Contracts are deliberately written in language that has meaning for legal situations and might have a completely different meaning in everyday use. As a project manager, you need to understand the contract to the best of your ability, but your job is to translate it into something that you can use to shape and define your project so that anyone in the company would then be able to understand and communicate the basic rationale for the project. The key is the translation. It is not always an easy job, but a necessary one for both planning and communication. Therefore, the contract becomes a key input document for developing the project charter.

Statement of the Business Problem

One of the best ways to align the project to business requirements is to put the business problem into your own words. In other words, paraphrase the problem as you understand it. If you cannot, it would be useful to talk with others who can help you. If you can think back to Chapter 1: Linking Projects to Strategy, the whole reason to sanction a plan in the first place is to improve performance. In this section of the charter, we want to make sure we establish that linkage and do it in a simple, yet direct, way. The value in taking the time to include this statement is that if you have somehow missed one important aspect of the problem, you are likely to open a discussion with your champion or sponsor to provide even more clarity. However, don't be surprised if occasionally they cannot articulate the problem very well.

In our MedTech case study, Rod Thompson, the project manager, developed this statement of the business problem: "We are using Project Renewal to better understand our customers and their buying requirements." The champion, Paula Dahlberg, thought that statement was too vague and suggested changing it to: "We are using Project Renewal to allow us to track and mine the data from our customers so we can grow our business with them." After reviewing the statement of the business problem with the sponsor, Lise Ramsay, she added these words to the end: ". . . and recognize opportunities for products and services they might require in the future."

As you can see, the development of the statement of the business problem allowed communications and dialogue between the three key people responsible for delivering the business value of the project—the project manager, the champion, and the sponsor—in that order. The discussion helped each one understand how the others were thinking about the project and ultimately allowed them to achieve an alignment of thought about what business problem this big initiative was to achieve as they started work. And the statement went from a vague and uninspiring sentence (Rod Thompson's first draft) to more complete, clear, and even a bit motivational description (provided by the champion, Paula Dahlberg, and the sponsor, Lise Ramsay). Without this exercise, it could have been months before they discovered that they were not in complete alignment on the outcome of the project. It also continues to draw the leadership into the project and keep them engaged.

Goals and Objectives for a Successful Project

The following statement is attributed to Benjamin Franklin: "By failing to prepare, you are preparing to fail." The point here is that part of the charter and the preparation for completing a project successfully is to determine how success will be measured. Establishing clear goals and objectives for the project will help everyone understand how they will be judged at its end.

The Primary Goals of Project Renewal

Every project has three primary goals:

1. To create something (in our case study a CRM system).
2. To complete it within a specific budgetary framework.
3. To finish it within an agreed-upon schedule.

Beyond these goals are others that must be specified and that actually define the project. MedTech's goals for Project Renewal were defined as the installation of a usable Customer Relationship Management system to

- Capture all customer profile information (e.g., addresses, locations, key personnel) accurately.
- Create reports that will allow the management and the marketing teams
  - To analyze each customer's history of purchases and whether incentive discounts affected buying patterns.
  - To predict future buying trends as an input to the research and development group for future product refinement.
  - To record and track credit limits and purchasing trends related to them.
- Allow the easy retrieval of all contracts with terms and conditions related to each customer's purchases.

The executive team decided that attempting to load all the historical data from the old legacy systems would be out of the scope of Project Renewal. They made the decision that trying to re-create the past would be too expensive for the potential value it might bring—which brings us to the communication of the project scope.

Project Scope

The scope statement within the project charter clearly defines what the project will and won't do. Many project managers believe that one key to a clearly defined scope is to detail what a project *will not* include as well as what it will include. The rationale for that is that most project managers will agree with their key stakeholders on what is included within the project, but will often diverge when it comes to what will not be included. For example, in our case study, the project manager and the champion agreed easily on most of the scope of what Project Renewal would include, but found they had some difficulty in agreeing on what would not be included. The project manager believed that the project did not include a record of items returned by customers for any variety of reasons (e.g., wrong product, wrong number of units delivered, unacceptable quality) because they had a system in place to capture that information. The champion, however, believed that was essential information to be captured and was part of the scope of the project. After meeting three times to resolve the problem with no success, they took their concerns to the sponsor. After each laid out arguments, the sponsor shared the information with the leadership team. The advantages of making this information a part of Project Renewal was clear—it provided more details about how a customer purchased from MedTech. The disadvantage was that it would take more time (and therefore money) to add capturing this data to the CRM. The leadership team debated and came back with a decision to include returned items within the scope of the project. Now imagine what would have happened if the project had moved forward for several months with no progress on capturing returned items within the CRM! Several key stakeholders could have been upset and all because the project manager started from a different assumption. Again, the charter discussion drove out a discussion that prevented that from happening.

Assumptions and Constraints

In this portion of the charter, the assumptions made about the completion of the project, details of any any assumptions that limit the project, or agreements that form the basis of interactions are listed here. Don't leave anything out that could affect the future management or successful completion of the project.

For example, in Project Renewal, Rod Thompson wrote the first draft of the charter and shared it with the Working Committee. He worked from the assumption that MedTech would be buying the Customer Relationship Management system "out of the box" with very little customization. However, Gary Stiles, the sales manager who sat on the Working Committee representing the sales department, objected. He insisted that there be more features than were included in the standard CRM. He also insisted that the CRM would require upgrading of the laptop computers the sales representatives used. Rod was working from the opposite side of both of those issues. To resolve the problem, both Rod and Gary made a presentation to the leadership team on the benefits each saw in his solution and the implications of accepting the position of the other. After deliberating on the subject, the leadership team decided that the project would not cover the cost of new laptops for the sales team. They would make provisions for that purchase out of a different budget item (which was clearly a win for Rod). However, they instructed Rod to make modifications to the CRM as long as they were not "major" modifications (a small victory for Gary). Unfortunately, they did not define exactly what a major modification was, so Rod had to navigate that passage with a minimum of guidance.

If you want the project to be considered a success, all side or off-line agreements must be approved in the charter—and, additionally, documented in this section. As for assumptions for Project Renewal, the project team assumed they must manage a complete retooling of the information management system, particularly the hardware and data connections. An example of a side or off-line agreement was the fact that the vendor has suggested that a new international tax module was scheduled for release about halfway through the project schedule. The agreement was this—if the module was delivered before the project finished, the project manager would provide the leadership team with an estimate of the extra money and time required to retrofit the module into the project and let them make a decision about whether to include it.

Risks and Benefits

In this portion, the charter will articulate the business benefits that the project expects to achieve and the risks to be managed based on an early understanding of the project. Benefits at this point are more likely to be qualitative rather than quantitative. The project manager can probably articulate a benefit that at the completion of the project, it will eliminate duplicate order entry problems (one order entry in the sales system and a second order entry required by the manufacturing system) in the old business process. However, if he were to attempt to provide an exact number, such as a reduction in order entry that equates to 4 hours per week per order, that would be so hypothetical that it probably would not be believed anyway. It is better that he just said it will only require one order entry and leave it at that during the early phase of the project.

Risk is defined as a measure of the probability and the consequence of not achieving the goals and objectives of the project.[2] In the early stages of a project, it is often hard to identify all the risks to the project, but some are obvious right from the beginning. Those are usually technical risks. For example, the CRM system will not work as advertised by the vendor. Most project managers, and Rod Thompson was no exception, focus on these risks and write them out in the project charter. Others are business risks and those are not so obvious. An example of a business risk that Rod and his team identified was that even if the CRM worked exactly as it should, the sales representatives would not keep the customer information current in it. However, I have to identify some risks that I believe too many project managers overlook— business risks that also may have an impact on the acceptance of a product or service once it makes it to operations. These risks include the following:

- **Lack of user acceptance:** The project has delivered what it promised from the technical side, but the users won't use it for any number of reasons.
- **Incompatibility with new business climate:** It will be a good project, and users will want it, but due to changes in the business marketplace, customers won't be able to afford it any longer.
- **Loss of political support:** If a project loses support from executive management, the whole project could be jeopardized. This might happen when a new executive is brought into a

---

[2]Ibid.

key position or loss of financial support occurs for any number of reasons.

The other idea to remember in developing your risk assessment is to write it in a fashion where others can understand the risk and the mitigation strategy you are proposing for that risk. Don't write a description of the risks the way that you might write them for the risk register. That level of detail that is too minute for a charter. Think of it this way—the risks you expose in the charter should be the big ones, the ones that can derail a project.

Project Budget and Schedule

As you can imagine, this is portion of the charter simply states the obvious: how much money you are expecting to spend and how much time you will take to complete the project. The level of detail will depend on the requirements of the business and you should check with your sponsor on how much detail the steering committee or governance board is expecting here. If you look at the Project Charter for Project Renewal in Figure 3.3, the budget is $15 million for a project duration of 24 months. At this stage of the plan, that is usually the level of detail that is possible.

Tips for Writing the Charter

The business world is moving toward writing what's easy to read and understand. Even diehards such as the armed forces and other government branches have joined progressive corporations in the move. The reasons for the change are clear—simple writing saves time, for both reader and writer (Figure 3.2). And it gets results you are looking for!

In each of the preferences, you are trying to simplify the written word so the readers can clearly understand your meaning. There are several key stakeholders, not to mention the project team members, who will need to understand the charter.

FIGURE 3.2 Use these tips for building understanding in the project charter.

To illustrate the point, read the following section from a project charter on the benefits achieved from one portion of a project.

> The asset built at the completion of the project effectively transfers all substantial risks to the customer with the rewards to the ownership of the Group and is to be included in tangible fixed assets and depreciated over the shorter of the term of the lease or its estimated useful life. The amount to be capitalized is the net present value, at the beginning of the lease, of the minimum payments to be made during the lease term exclusive of revenue items such as maintenance and insurance. Outstanding obligations due under such a lease, net of finance charges, are to be included as a third party loan liability. The finance element of the rental payments is to be charged to the profit and loss account over the term of the lease.

I ask you, how easy is it to understand the wording in this portion of this charter? It could be simplified and worded so that others besides accountants and lawyers could understand it.

Statement of the Business Problem	MedTech is using Project Renewal to allow us to have all the information on our customers in one place to better track and mine the data we have on our customers so we can grow our business with them and recognize opportunities for products and services they might require in the future.

Goals and Objectives	• Capture all customer profile information (e.g., addresses, locations, key personnel) accurately.
	• Create reports that will allow the management team and the marketing team
	  • To analyze each customer's history of purchases and whether incentive discounts affected their buying patterns.
	  • To predict future buying trends as an input to the research and development group for future product development.
	  • To record and track credit limits and purchasing trends related to those limits.
	• Allow the easy retrieval of all contracts with terms and conditions related to each customer's purchases.

Project Scope	The scope of the project includes the successful installation, implementation, and sustained use of a Customer Relationship Management software program. The software will also replace the current program for customer returns of products and the reasons for the returns. The project will not include any changes or recommendations related to sales territories.
Assumptions and Constraints	• A complete retooling of the information management system, particularly the hardware and data connections, will be required. • The project team assumes that the laptop computers used by the sales and marketing staff will not be replaced using the budget for this project. • The CRM software can be installed with few modifications to meet the needs of MedTech and will not include any major customization. • The vendor has suggested that a new international tax module is scheduled for release about halfway through the project schedule. If the module is delivered before the project finishes, the project manager will provide the leadership team an estimate of the extra money and time required to retrofit the module into the project prior to any decision related to the new module.
Budget and Schedule	• Budget: $15M for installation, licensing, and hardware • Schedule: 24 months from the sanctioning of the project to completion

FIGURE 3.3 The Project Charter for Project Renewal was written to communicate with key stakeholders in clear, concrete language.

For writing any documents, whether the charter or documents related to your project, there are three key preferences to keep in mind: Prefer the

1. Concrete to the abstract.
2. Single word to the phrase.
3. Short word to the long one.

Each of these preferences allows the reader to get to the point quickly. People are bombarded daily by messages and written materials in all forms—the worst being the avalanche of email. They won't take the time to fight through difficult writing. These three preferences make it easy to simplify the writing and allow your readers to meet you mentally.

The project charter that Rod Thompson developed for Project Renewal is shown in Figure 3.3.

Key Points to Remember

- The project charter is a written document for communicating with key stakeholders to ensure alignment at the start of the project.
- The charter fundamentals should contain the key discussion points between the project manager and those same key stakeholders.

So the development of the project charter is a key to effective communications with major stakeholders. However, there is another key group to communicate with—and with far more regularity and clarity—the project team members! In the next chapter, let's look at how some of these same communication concepts can be used in communicating with the team.

Chapter 4

Establishing the Team and Communicating with the Business

In the previous chapter, we looked at how the project charter can be used as a communication document with key stakeholders. In this chapter, let's look at two key communication concepts related to the project team members:

1. Using your team members as a communication vehicle with the key stakeholders.
2. Understanding the basics of communicating with your team.

In thinking about establishing your team, there are the usual considerations such as

- Who is available?
- What skills and experience do they have?
- What roles (such as technical, business analyst) will you need them to fill as part of the project?

Another key question you might consider asking yourself is, would some of my key roles, such as technical team lead, be able to connect and communicate with key stakeholders?

Rod Thompson asked himself that question in staffing his team. It was a key reason that Rod wanted Luke Johnson on the team as liaison with the Information Technology group. He knew that Luke was both liked and respected by Dan Cohen, the Director of the IT group. Rod recognized that Project Renewal would need both help and cooperation from the IT group as it progressed. Luke would be a key person in communicating with those IT people when work started on such tasks as building the interface between the CRM and the data management portion of Dan's group. Luke's ability to communicate with these technical people could prevent problems that might be created by misunderstandings, plus it could help to solve problems when they arose later on in the project.

Communicating the Sale

In many cases, project managers are not involved in the sale of the project. However, all project managers must be aware that there is still a "sale" to be made to various stakeholders affected by the results of the initiative. Let's identify these affected people as "buyers." What are they buying? They are buying the idea that your project will actually benefit them personally. The central concept is that the "sale" is not finished just because a Project Charter has been signed or agreed to.

Rod Thompson recognized this fact. He began to identify various people as one of three types of "buyer" he had to sell: economic buyers, technical buyers, and user buyers.

> Economic buyers are those who are providing the funds for the project and expect to see the business benefits. Technical buyers are those who must be convinced that the project solution will solve the technical problem. And the user buyers are those who will actually use the deliverables as part of their day-to-day work.

Rod identified Lise Ramsay as the economic buyer since she was the executive who both pushed for the CRM and also become the sponsor for the project. He identified Paula Dahlberg, the Director of Marketing, Gary Stiles, Sales Manager, and Walter Fisher, General Manager of Manufacturing, as the technical buyers. Their departments were the most impacted by the changes resulting from Project Renewal. In most cases, but not all, the economic buyers and the technical buyers must be satisfied with the project as defined or it would not be sanctioned and funded. However, the user buyers are very often left out of the discussions until the decision has been reached. They are compelled to go along with the project, but are far from enthusiastic. The user buyers for this initiative were all the people within Paula's, Gary's, and Walter's departments who would actually be using the CRM to input information and produce reports and data. Other people might also use the CRM, but these were, by far, the largest and most important groups. Rod realized the "sale" to this latter group must continue throughout the project to make sure the deal was really "closed." He determined that communications would be the key to keeping the sale.

All projects and project managers use teams of people to assist in completing the project. However, they often focus on the technical side of the project and do not engage the business in the development of the team. When you are establishing communications inside your project team, you will need to help your team members understand that you really have two parallel tracks progressing simultaneously (Figure 4.1). One track is keeping people in the business informed about what is happening and when. The second track is providing the project team with information that allows them to stay in touch with the people—particularly the user buyers. The key concept is making sure the project team is providing the same information to the business as you are!

One of the basics for establishing a project team is to conduct a stakeholder analysis related to the project team. We'll look at a stakeholder analysis related to specifics on communications later on in Chapter 5. However, it is important to consider various

FIGURE 4.1 Parallel communication tracks.

stakeholders in staffing your project team because the interaction, including effective communications, will be critical to the ultimate success of your project. We will look at the communication plan in Chapter 10.

One of the first steps in planning the way your team members will communicate with the business people will be to consider these realities:

> Stakeholders are defined as people who have a vested interest in the outcome of a project, even if they do not fund or participate in the project directly.

- Relationship of these key business people with each other.
- Level of knowledge of the goals and business case for the project.
- Credibility the project team will need with these key individuals.
- Concerns or questions key business people might have on the details.
- Information or techniques to gain acceptance with them.

Let's take a look at each of these elements.

Relationship with Each Other

When you analyze the various business people who will be interacting with the project team members, one of the key concerns will always be how the politics within the company play out. Before you or your team members begin communicating with various departments, you will need to discover who reports to whom. An organization chart is useful, but as companies get more complex, its use may be limited. However, you will need to pass along that information to your project team members and make sure they are following the correct protocol in talking with business people. For example, Rod Thompson made sure his team leads, Paul Ryan on the business side and Josh Larsen on the technical side, knew that they were not to discuss various problems with users in different departments UNTIL they had spoken to their supervisors first. It was frowned upon within MedTech for a staff person to know something before his or her manager did (that's what I mean by protocol). There are also significant people who influence others but are not on the organization chart with management authority. You and your team need to find out who those people are. There is always a corporate culture to deal with as well. The rules for culture are not found in the company handbook or initiation seminar. They are the unwritten rules about the way things are done within a company. And using the correct protocol is part of that culture. These basics will become even more important later when we discuss Developing Support for New Business Processes in Chapter 8.

Level of Knowledge of the Goals and Business Case

It may surprise you to know that often the rationale for a project and the expected business case are not widely known beyond a few key individuals. While it may seem obvious, as a project manager, you may be the person who educates key individuals on the goals the project is attempting to achieve. That is why the development of the Case for Change will be important (you'll learn more about the Case for Change in Chapter 6). If that is true, think of how important it is that your project team members know and understand the goals and business case for the endeavor. Of course, use your judgment in this—for example, the programmers for Project Renewal don't need a thorough understanding of the business case. Just make sure that those members of your team who do need to know are informed.

Credibility of the Project Team

Often a project team will be a mixture of inside people seconded to the project and outsiders. The insiders can be nominated for a variety of reasons, some good and some bad. If you are receiving people because they "are available," it may be that you don't have the best players the departments have to offer. If they are people who are considered "stars" within the organization and they are nominated to your project because of the knowledge and experience they can bring, you will not have the same struggle with credibility. If you are also hiring contractors or consultants from the outside, you will need to spend more time on the section a little later in the chapter on what to look for in these critical members of your project team.

Questions or Concerns

Often in critical projects people will still have questions or concerns about how things are going to work after the project is complete. The problem a project manager faces in this situation is that you won't have the details for a while. However, it will be important to understand these questions and concerns, document them, and as you make progress in addressing them, communicate with those key individuals to fill them in on the details.

Information or Techniques to Gain Acceptance

Generally speaking, people will fall into two camps related to the way they receive and accept information:

1. Focusing on the details of the changes the project will bring.
2. Focusing on how people will respond to the changes the project will foster.

Providing individuals with the correct "type" of information is as important as the communication itself. The first group seems pretty obvious, but perhaps not the second. I once had a client who always asked me the same question when I approached him about project issues or decisions. It went something like this: "Who is going to be mad at me about this decision/issue?" It was rarely "Why did you do that?" or "What other options did you consider?"

Communications Within the Team

There are a variety of ways to foster and support communications within the team. Here are a few that we'll look at in more detail:

- Team building
- Team meetings
- War room management

Team Building

Teams are built when they all share and support the same goal (to complete a successful project). We might think about using the theatre as a way to think about building a great team. Actors, great and small, generally follow the lead of the director, and each player does his or her best to fulfill the specific role assigned in each play. Even the stars must follow the rules of the game. You are the director, and your team members are the actors. People on your project team need to play their roles in the same way.

For the people working on your project to become a real team, some specific things need to happen with your coaching and leadership as project manager. Project members need to

- Realize they'll be working on activities that involve more than one person. Therefore, they'll need to communicate and cooperate with each other to get things done.
- Share common methods and tools for assessing and communicating the status of the project.

- Identify and solve problems together and then live with the results (together) and agree to support the common decision in public.
- Accept the fact that, if one person makes a mistake, the entire team suffers. Therefore, members need to help each other avoid as many mistakes as possible.
- Realize that new people will be joining and other people will be leaving the project as time goes on, but the overall team structure and project goals will remain the same until the project reaches fruition.
- Recognize that changes will occur, and they must be flexible enough to adjust and use the change control methods that are described in much more detail in Chapter 9.

When other organizations or departments are involved, positive interaction between the project manager and these organizations is also critical to creating a good team. The relationships among line, staff, vendors, customers, and project personnel must be tempered with mutual trust. Make sure that you emphasize these ideas over and over again with your project team.

Communicating During Meetings

Here are some key ideas for communicating effectively in meetings during your project.

Always have a specific purpose for any meeting you arrange. To be frank, I don't consider "to provide the champion with information" to be a valid reason, and members are not likely to appreciate that purpose either. A much better purpose might be "to get your advice on how to handle an issue related to the input of customer data by sales." If you are asking for time with the sponsor or champion to achieve that outcome, your meeting will in-

> When you are asking the champion, or sponsor, to help you solve a problem, always remember his or her effective span of authority and don't ask him or her to "solve" a problem outside of that scope. A better request if it is outside a person's authority is to ask that it be escalated to the management team as one example.

form him or her (because you will need to provide background information), but you are asking someone to tackle a problem. Most managers appreciate being called on to handle that type of issue.

Always use a structured agenda for managing project team meetings and track

> The "parking lot" handles items that are outside the agenda of the meeting. Before the end of the meeting, decide when and how you will handle each item entered on the parking lot.

- Date, time, location, and people in attendance.
- Decisions made during the meeting.
- Actions assigned to people and the target date for completion.
- Issues or risks identified and closed.
- Items placed in the parking lot for the future.

Always provide meeting minutes (Figure 4.2).

Project Renewal Team Meeting Minutes

Date: 02/06/2008
Time: 2:30 - 3:30 P.M.
Chair: Paula Dahlberg, champion
Attendees: Rod Thompson   Anne Garcia
Leeland Olson   Dan Cohen
Carrie Jenkins   Gary Stiles (by phone)
Walter Fisher

Decisions:
Agreed on the Case for Change and for the project.

Items:	Person Responsible	Date	Status
Action Items:			
Research billing requirements for accounts receivable	Leeland Olson	12/06/2007	Completed
Investigate the credit policy as requested by the project team	Leeland Olson	12/06/2007	Completed
Review requirements for new order input with scheduling	Walter Fisher	1/19/2008	In progress
Submit RFP for new servers	Dan Cohen	1/19/2006	In progress

Parking Lot:
Data storage and data mining   Parked until late February

FIGURE 4.2 An example of meeting minutes captured after one of the project meetings for Project Renewal.

Managing the War Room

I'm not sure if everyone uses this term in project management, but when I refer to the war room, I am referring to a conference room or other similar facility that is reserved for the use of the project team during the course of a project. You can use the war room as a communication tool as well as a work space.

For example, you should keep timelines visible to anyone walking by or coming to visit you or another of your team members. You would be surprised how many people are not familiar with your project schedule and become "educated" by seeing it on the war room wall.

Another great communication tactic is to make key project team members available to end users through visits to the war room. Let your team members know that you are encouraging them to meet in the war room unless it is reserved for a specific project activity such as a standing meeting.

You may also choose to communicate by inviting key stakeholders to meetings in the war room. Allowing these key people to see where the project team is working can often make them feel more comfortable in approaching the team members, or you, when they have certain issues of concerns. This can also serve as one of the feedback mechanisms for your communications plan that can help you to address rumors immediately.

Having provided you with several ideas in the use of the war room, there are several warnings that are very important to remember. First of all, any confidential information regarding the project or people associated with the project should be kept elsewhere under lock and key and not in the war room, if possible.

The final warning is to watch for rogue project team members and the messages they are providing to key stakeholders or users, whether inside or outside the war room. There is nothing that can destroy the confidence of your users or stakeholders more than hearing that the project is a mess from one of the members of the project team. Deal with those types of project team members swiftly and firmly. You will need to listen to them (I'll talk more about listening in a minute), but you cannot have a project team member giving information to others that contradicts the "official" message that you are providing to key stakeholders. I won't tell you that it is easy to deal with these situations, because it is not. However, you severely increase the risk that your project will fail if confidence is eroded by these rogue project team members.

Listening Is Part of Communicating

The ability to listen is one of the most important communication skills a project manager can possess. Only through listening can you determine whether your communications are understood the way you intended them to be understood. Figure 4.3 shows a model of basic communication.

Focused listening helps keep you informed about how people associated with your project are thinking—better than any status

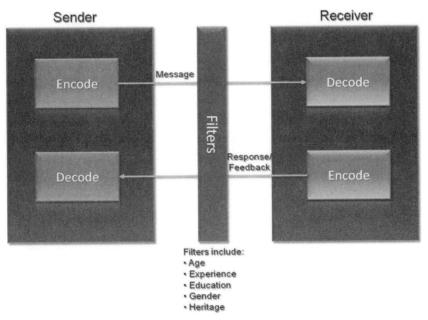

FIGURE 4.3 Simple communications model.

report. Observant listening can also help you foresee political issues before they start bogging down the project.

Here are some tips for becoming a better listener:

- Stop talking and let others tell you what they want to say.
- Let people finish what they are saying. Try not to interrupt before the person finishes because you'll never hear any person's complete intent if you do. If there is a brief pause in the discussion, don't jump in prematurely. Allow the other person to finish before you take your turn.
- Eliminate as many distractions as possible, such as telephone calls, cell phones, or people coming in and out of the office. Give the person your full attention.
- Listen with purpose and intent. Try to hear between the words for the underlying meaning of the message. Notice body language and facial expressions as people talk. These are often the clues to dissatisfaction or issues that are not being addressed. If you see something wrong in the person's face, ask some probing questions to get at the real concerns.
- Restate or summarize what you hear people say to make sure you have understood the message correctly. Only by both receiving and understanding the message can good communication occur.

Remember that the best predictors of a successful project are

1. Robust communication between the project team and the stakeholders.
2. Strong communications within the project team itself.

Key Points to Remember

- There is still a "sale" to be made in every project.

- Different people will have varying understanding about the project, and one approach to communications will not fit everyone.
- As much as possible, choose the key members of your project team based on their ability to communicate effectively and knowledgably with the business people.
- Establish strong communications within the project team as well as between the project and the customers.

Now that the definition phase of the project is completed, we now move into the planning phase. In this phase, there will be a great deal of communications to plan. The good news is that whether writing, speaking, or meeting, there are some common communication elements regardless of the situation. That is where we will go next!

Chapter 5

Common Elements
for All Communications

The secret for all the types of communications, whether written (such as emails or reports) or verbal (such as presentations or town hall meetings), that a project manager would use during the course of a project can be summarized in three steps:

1. Analyze the target.
2. Plan the approach.
3. Deliver the message.

Since these steps apply to almost any communication situation, I will cover those universal steps, then refer back to them in later chapters in the book. They are universal steps because you must at least consider them when you prepare any important communication related to your project. You may not necessarily use them, but you ignore them at your own peril. First, I present a quick overview of what they are, followed by a more detailed description regarding their application during a project.

Step One: Analyze the Target

Stakeholder Analysis

When determining the target for any communications, the first consideration has to be who will receive the messages. For that, you will need to identify who the stakeholders are for the project. The Project Management Institute defines stakeholders as those people who "are actively involved in the project, or whose interests may be affected by as a result of the project completion or execution."[1] The entire foundation for building a communication plan stems from an understanding of whom you are communicating to.

As you can see from Figure 5.1, the project communication plan is at the center of the interaction between and among all the stakeholders—from the executive management to the end users. By targeting the messages to their distinct needs and concerns, you can create alignment as well as understanding.

FIGURE 5.1   At a high level, these are the key groups of people impacted by the project.

---

[1]*Project Management Body of Knowledge* (Newton Square, PA: Project Management Institute, 2003), section 2.2, page 24.

When beginning a stakeholder analysis, a simple guide is often very useful to lead the discussions and assist the project manager in clarifying the perspectives and concerns of all the people associated with the project. The stakeholder analysis guide in Figure 5.2 can steer you in asking the right questions. Your particular situation might cause you to alter the questions, or add other questions, but appreciate that this is almost the minimum information that any project manager will require to build a communication plan.

The value of this kind of analysis for project managers like Rod Thompson, our MedTech Project Renewal project manager,

Question	Response
Who are the key individuals who care about the work that will be affected by the project? (see examples below) ■ Sales ■ Customer Relations ■ Manufacturing ■ Vendor management and contracts ■ Marketing ■ Senior Management Team	
What are their responsibilities related to Project Renewal?	
What do they know about the project already?	
Who knows about the project and can help us to understand the situation?	
Who doesn't know about the project and what information will they require?	
Who is likely to dislike any ideas for change? What will they dislike about those changes?	
What information and techniques are most likely to be accepted by these stakeholders?	
How will we best manage their expectations for the project?	

FIGURE 5.2   Stakeholder analysis tool.

is the insights it provides into who will support the type of changes the project will produce and who will oppose them. As part of Project Renewal, Rod knew that a feature of the CRM software allowed a customer to view the progress of its order as it was being processed by MedTech. In determining the impact a feature like that might have, he realized he did not have the answers to some of these questions. He needed to find someone who did. The logical choice was the champion, Paula Dahlberg. The champion can also review any assessments made related to this analysis and provide feedback on those assessments. As for the question related to the information and techniques for communicating, it seeks to help Rod understand how to be persuasive in his communications. People tend to fall into two camps relative to persuasive information. One camp is only impressed by data, and the other camp is mostly concerned with how people will react to changes or suggestions for change. For example, in Project Renewal, Paula explained to Rod that Walter Fisher, the Manufacturing Manager, was only impressed by facts and data. Rod realized that in discussing issues and information related to the online customer viewing of orders, he had better have data and facts when talking to Walter. However, Paula also knew that Carrie Jenkins, the Customer Relations Manager, was usually concerned about how people (in particular, customers) would react to certain ideas that create changes. The same information that Rod would provide Walter would not be received very well by Carrie. For her, he would need to be prepared to discuss how he believed customers would react to a feature like that. Rod realized that he would need to communicate to these two key stakeholders very differently over the course of the project—he had to make sure he hit the target. Like many things in life, the concept of one-size-fits-all doesn't work very well in project communications.

Purpose of the Communication

The second key to correctly targeting your communications is to determine what you are trying to achieve with that communication—its purpose. To define your purpose, it is important to remember that any important communication related to your project should work to achieve one of these four broad objectives:

1. Instruction: Informing or teaching people something.
2. Inspiration: Motivating your readers or listeners to act in a certain way.
3. Advocating: Convincing or selling someone on your point of view.
4. Stimulation: Stimulating discussion or debate.[2]

At any time during the course of the project, you will use at least one of these objectives during each communication.

The best way I know to think about your purpose is to finish the following statement: "The purpose of this communication is . . . ." Believe me when I tell you that if you can't finish that statement, those who read your note or listen to your presentation won't be able to decipher the purpose either!

In our MedTech case study, Rod Thompson made a decision that the purpose of his next communication to senior management would be to stimulate a discussion and the attendant decision around who was going to be accountable for any inaccurate data for customer orders after the CRM was working and Project Renewal was completed. As a result, he worked with Paula Dahlberg, the champion, to draft a status report for the senior management that would be presented by Lise Ramsay, the sponsor. Since the issue cut across several departments, it was absolutely an issue that needed senior management input and/or resolution. In the report, they suggested that based on the lack of agreement on this subject within the Working Committee, a possible alternative was to hire order entry clerks to ensure that the proper information was entered into the CRM. Based on the current level of orders and the expected increase after Project Renewal was operational, he estimated

---

[2]G. Michael Campbell, *Bulletproof Presentations* (Franklin Lakes, NJ: Career Press, 2002), p. 14.

that MedTech would require an additional 50 people to fill these new positions. As you can imagine, that got the attention of senior management! They immediately questioned key members of the Working Committee, and Rod had an answer to the question within a week. The important point was that Rod had a purpose—to stimulate discussion and drive a decision—and developed the communication to achieve that purpose.

Step Two: Plan the Approach

After you have completed an analysis of the target for the communication and clearly defined the purpose, you now have to plan the approach that will best achieve your purpose with a particular target audience.

Strategy

One can employ several strategies in presenting information to stakeholders. Here is a summary of the common strategies:

- *Most critical to least critical* is useful where a series of variables have had an impact on the outcome of the decisions related to the project. Start with the most critical and move to the least critical or more common elements. An example might be explaining to management the criteria the project team used for choosing a vendor. You might have determined that certain characteristics such as reliability, relationship with your company, and experience of the vendor consultants were the most important in choosing a vendor—the most critical in the decision. Other characteristics, such as price and after-installation service. were less critical because all the vendors seemed to be fairly equal.
- *Problem/solution* is often used in technical situations where the project is solving various issues, and the resolutions to those problems are addressed in the communication. A variation of this strategy is *question/answer*, where a particular

communication addresses the questions people have in their minds and the provides the answers.

- *Big picture/small picture* helps those who are receiving the communication to understand how you are applying the data and information you have gathered to meet the larger goals of the company. This is usually very persuasive with senior management, who are usually concerned with the big picture. For example, in Project Renewal, Rod Thompson used this approach to explain the decisions around customer reporting made by the project team and the Working Committee. Since the strategy of the company is to grow (the big picture), he demonstrated how the reports would allow management to see growth by customers in a wide variety of ways (the small picture).

- *Compare/contrast* can be a very effective strategy when communicating how a particular project might be similar to one that people are familiar with (compare) and how it might differ (contrast). This strategy can allow you to stress the differentiation that would be important to the stakeholders receiving the communication. This might be very important if a similar project had been attempted in the past and failed. You would want to clarify how your project is different from the failed project even though they might appear similar on the surface.

There is no right strategy for any single communication. The best policy is to choose one that suits your purpose for communication and fits the expectations of the stakeholders you are trying to reach.

Politics and Communication

There is probably not a single project manager today who hasn't had to carefully navigate the political waters surrounding a project. Politics is a very important consideration when planning your communications; it is always important to consider opinions and beliefs and how they will affect your ability to achieve your purpose. There are two key sources of power that you will need to concern yourself with. The first is authority, and the second is expertise. Both of these sources of influence are obvious but often overlooked by project managers when communicating. If we go back to Rob Thompson's purpose in the previous example, he made the decision that authority was the source for the muscle he needed to make sure the communication (the CRM reporting) achieved its objective—to stimulate discussion and drive the executive team to a decision. If the communication had required a level of technical knowledge, then perhaps he would have used a member of the Working Committee to deliver the message.

In addition, you would need to consider who has a vested interest in the status quo or who would lose power or authority as the result of changes brought about by the project. You will need to craft any messages carefully related to any of these issues or pay the consequences, which usually means finding yourself in the middle of a political struggle.

Usually, one of the best sources for understanding the corporate landscape is the sponsor. In our MedTech case study, Lise Ramsay is an officer and will deal with all of the top officers on a regular basis. Rod used Lise regularly to make sure the tone of his communications wasn't going to ruffle any feathers in the executive suite.

Formal or Informal

The command structure within the organization will also dictate how formal the requirements are for various communications. Since Rod's communication to drive discussion and decision was going all the way up the organization to the senior management, the message that he and Paula developed needed to be fairly formal. This formality required a memo that was very clear and concise in its content with the correct level of detail for this group of executives. An email message to this troupe would be received very badly as too informal. However, an informal note via email may be very appropriate for a different message targeted for the staff people within the accounting department. The level of formality is also influenced by the corporate culture—how formal (or informal) it is. Always be cognizant of the formality that might be required for any communications and aim for that level.

Barriers to Communications

There will always be obstacles to communications. These hurdles may come in various forms: on a macro level, such as geography, language, culture, and on a micro level, such as technical definitions or jargon used in communications. In his communications plan, Rod Thompson was also working with MedTech people from Europe and Singapore. In planning various communications with key stakeholders, he needed to keep in mind a variety of barriers. As examples of just one—time zones:

- The facility in France was 7 hours ahead of his location in the central United States.
- Singapore was 14 hours ahead and often on the next calendar day when he was working.

When it came to language barriers, the good news for Rod was that as a rule, English is the global language of business these days. Therefore, he could develop his communications in English and not worry about providing translations in most cases. However, he had to remember to keep his language concrete and direct. He also had to guard against using American slang or colloquial expressions because they might not translate very well for people whose first language is not English. Even folks in the British office might scratch their heads if he used a phrase from the American West such as "that dog won't hunt" to mean an idea that would not be accepted. Everyone would clearly understand the words, but they would not understand the meaning.

Then there is the natural jargon and shorthand language used in business today. All companies have their own expressions.

Certain departments have them too. Jargon and acronyms have a place in organizations because they allow people to take shortcuts to certain common ideas or concepts. However, jargon is also a way to exclude and make others feel on the outside. If Rod used the jargon from Information Technology to explain how the customer data within the CRM can be retrieved by users, he would construct a barrier between himself and his readers or listeners. The best approach for Rod to take was to draft his message, and then ask several members of the Working Committee to review it. He would ask them to make sure he was using appropriate language and had not used jargon that he would later have to explain—or could be misunderstood. Often these Working Committee members would provide suggestions for wording ideas in a way that the audience would understand and appreciate. In addition to clarity, Rod was building credibility with the key stakeholders because he communicated to them in their own language.

Step Three: Deliver the Message

Tools and Technology

A wide variety of tools exist for project managers to use in communicating with team members and key stakeholders. For example, Rod had asked all of his team members to use instant messenger technology. The goal was to allow everyone to "chat" with each other quickly even if they were separated by significant barriers of time or distance. It was often quicker and easier than a telephone call. However, he developed a guideline that stated if an IM session lasted more than two or three lines, he wanted people to pick up the telephone and call. For example, when Anne Garcia needed to confirm the meeting location for the business analysts, a quick instant message to Paul Ryan was appropriate. However, if the simple question spun into a discussion of the topics to be covered in the meeting, then it was time for Anne to pick up the phone and call Paul.

There are also online meeting services that allow several people to share and view the same documents in real time. By using a conference call arrangement for the audio portion, Rod could have a virtual meeting with a widely dispersed group of people, including a review of the project plan. The beauty of these tools was that he could make changes to documents during the course of the meeting, and everyone could see and agree to the alterations in real time. He recognized that this tool saved him from taking notes and then circulating the changes and waiting for others to confirm. Also, many of these online meeting providers have the capability to record the meeting. That can be valuable for team members who miss the meeting due to schedule conflicts, illness, or vacation time. If what was missed was important, that team member could call up the recording of the meeting and listen to the entire session after the fact. Rod decided that he would record any meeting where decisions were on the agenda. He wanted to make sure that if questions or disagreements occurred later on in the project, everyone could review the meeting, including the actual recording, to illustrate the consensus on the discussions and the final outcome. He found that to be even more effective than written minutes of the meetings.

Four Rules for Communication

In developing your communications, you must remember the Four Rules for Communications.[3] They are:

- Rule of Frequency
- Rule of Primacy
- Rule of Recency
- Rule of Emotion

The Rule of Frequency states that people will remember information they have heard more frequently. This is the basis for multiple mailings from advertisers—and why they repeat commercials on TV frequently. Advertisers recognize that it takes multiple

---

[3]Ibid., pp. 22–23.

times to break through to your consciousness. Therefore, in communicating important information such as the Case for Change, you must recognize that one time will not be enough for people to remember it!

The Rule of Primacy states that people remember well the first time they heard about something. For you, it means people will remember the first time they heard about your project and it sets a mental "benchmark" in their mind about the intiative. It means that you must be very careful with the initial message because it will become the yardstick for all the others you send. Therefore, take care and perhaps use a specialist like Rod did when he brought Anna Garcia into the project team.

The Rule of Recency states that people will remember the most recent information they hear and compare it to previous announcements for any inconsistencies. As we all recognize, things may change over the course of a project, particularly one with a long duration. The point is to be sure to explain any changes because if you do not, people will begin to speculate as to why things have changed and you have not explained it. Speculation of that nature can only damage the project in the eyes of the users.

The Rule of Emotion states that people remember information that impacts them emotionally. In the case of Project Renewal, people within MedTech remembered information when it explained how their job or performance reviews would be affected. While you can't back off from any changes, you need to be sensitive to the situation. I will talk more about sensitivities in Chapter 10: Developing the Communications for the Project.

Oral Versus Written Communications

The 3M Corporation conducted a series of studies to determine the effectiveness of using different delivery techniques to get people to remember information.[4] They determined that people remember

---

[4]Ibid., p. 167.

- 10 percent of what they read.
- 20 percent of what they hear.
- 30 percent of what they see.
- 60 percent of what they see, hear, and read!

The study should provide us with ample evidence that if we want our key stakeholders, including our project team members, to remember what we have communicated, we must use a combination of written and oral communication. Only using one or the other introduces another risk into our project.

Role Descriptions and Communications

Whenever there is communication between members of the project team and the business (or key stakeholders), clearly defined role descriptions can help immensely (see Figure 5.3).

In Project Renewal, if Dan Cohen, as the Director of IT, had a question or concern, he knew that he needed to talk with Luke Johnson because Luke's role was liaison with IT. That was not to say he couldn't talk to other team members, but Dan was clear that Luke had that responsibility.

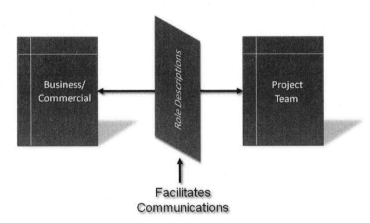

FIGURE 5.3   Role descriptions can help facilitate the communication between the project team and the business.

Key Points to Remember

- All communications begin with a stakeholder analysis.
- Identify the purpose of any message.
- Plan the strategy that best achieves the purpose.
- Pinpoint the method for delivering any communication.

In summary, there are some common elements for all types of communications to be developed during a project. It does not matter whether they are written or oral, large group or small group, the basics are the same.

Utilizing these common building blocks of communication are very important in drafting the Case for Change—the simple, yet direct explanation of why you are doing a project in the first place. The next chapter will discuss the importance of this document to the diffusion of information about your venture.

Chapter 6

Writing the Case for Change

Any project that impacts a large number of people creates the need for communications. Many times project managers are at a loss about where to begin. If one reviews documents like the financial business case and even the charter, there is really only limited help to be found. Instead, begin one of the best exercises you and the key stakeholders for your project will ever do together: Develop a Case for Change. The Case for Change is a simple document, written in plain English, that explains the rationale for the project.

Most people impacted by a project have a natural inclination

> In successful large-scale change, a well-functioning guiding team answers the questions required to produce a clear sense of direction. Good answers . . . position an organization to leap into a better future.
>
> *John P. Kotter and Dan S. Cohen,* The Heart of Change[1]

---

[1]John P. Kotter and Dan S. Cohen, *The Heart of Change* (Cambridge, MA: Harvard Business School Press, 2002), pp. 61, 84.

to ask "Why are we doing this project?" The Case for Change is developed to address that basic question, but ultimately it serves several other purposes as well. So what is the secret to writing a case for change?

What Is the Secret to Writing a Case for Change?

Here are some general guidelines for developing the Case for Change. First of all, work with your project team and the business sponsor to answer the following questions:

1. Why are we doing this project from a business perspective?
2. What will change when the project is completed?
3. What will happen if we don't complete this project successfully?
4. What are the benefits of doing this project to us and the business?
5. What will we need to do differently?

Feel free to edit these questions as appropriate for your project and your situation. These are all common questions that the vast majority of people impacted by a project are asking themselves, and others, each time a new initiative is proposed by management. As project manager, you need to engage the key business leaders to answer these questions. Please realize that they may not be able to answer them in the everyday language of the business. They may tend to give you language that is typical of the standard business case (I'll talk more about this later in the chapter).

Influences on Behavior

What the project manager is attempting to do is to influence the behaviors of the users of our project deliverables (see Figure 6.1). These behaviors are the actions used by individuals to complete the

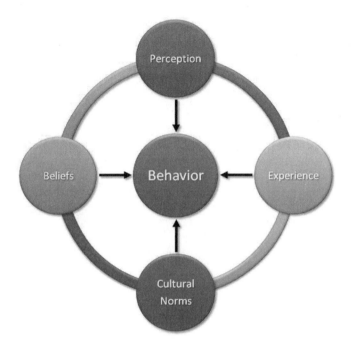

FIGURE 6.1   Influencing behavior.

work that comprises their job. Several elements influence conduct, including beliefs, cultural norms, experience, and perception. This is the context we must understand when we hand off our project deliverables to operations. For example, a project will not be sustainable after completion if it requires behavior that is highly individualistic (make a decision to provide a customer a financial refund) in a company culture that values command and control (in the past only senior managers could make those decisions). Any person who is now asked to provide refunds would be highly suspicious of any requirements that asked him

> Culture is a set of norms related to shared values and behaviors in a group of people. It defines what the group values and how members should act. If individuals in the group stray from the norms, their peers within the group will give them feedback, without even thinking about it, either directly through words or indirectly through body language, to return to the normal behavior.

or her to make that decision in the future. As you can imagine, this person would want ironclad assurance there would be no negative repercussions.

Unfortunately, as project managers we have very little impact on people's beliefs and experience. And we can only understand the cultural norms that influence people so we can be sensitive to those norms as we prepare operations for the project deliverables.

Communications Create Perception

However, we can have a strong influence on their perception of reality with a robust communications plan for our project. So how can we influence people's impressions? Fair question! First, let's look at the classic model for how people develop their views on things (Figure 6.2).

People arrive at an opinion by going through a process of acquiring information, then interpreting it, selecting the portions they find useful, and then organizing it to make sense of the awareness they now have.

The way to illustrate the situation a project manager can face associated with perception is to recount what happens to police officers when they interview witnesses to an auto accident. If there are five people involved, the officer is likely to hear five different interpretations of what happened. If a project manager keeps this state of affairs in mind, he or she won't allow the normal chaos of life to recreate a similar variation of interpretations for his or her proj-

FIGURE 6.2   Classic process of perception.

ect. Using effective communications, the project team is controlling and influencing

1. How people affected by the impact of the project acquire their facts.
2. The way people interpret the data by providing the correct translation so they understand it.
3. The evidence for people so they don't have to sort through a variety of useless garbage to find the pieces useful to them.
4. The organization of the information into knowledge so it is easily structured and organized by the audience to the desired result.

By using this model, the perception of the users about what is happening is controlled and influenced to drive the behavior we need to make the project a success when we hand it over to on-going operations.

In many cases, the people who are impacted, directly or indirectly, will be reluctant to change from what they know to some unknown (to them) solution. And they will quite naturally fear that the "cure" will be worse than the problem itself. Many project managers of information technology projects have faced that resistance when they implemented a software package that would replace their use of spreadsheets for capturing and manipulating data. Their reluctance is based on the fact that they have built the spreadsheets themselves so they trust them. They are not sure they can trust another tool as much. The Case for Change is designed to address those concerns at a high level.

> The key is one basic insight: Good communications is not just data transfer.
>
> *John P. Kotter and Dan S. Cohen*[2]

Remember to use words that will resonate with the people the project impacts. Nothing will turn them off faster than using language that is "project speak" (such as "deliverables" and "Statement of Work") or "consultant speak" (such as "synergy" and "leverage")—well, you get the idea. That

---

[2]Ibid.

is where your business sponsor or business Working Committee members can help.

Process for Building a Case for Change

The project team should develop a first draft, and then the Working Committee or end users can edit it. When you start to draft this document, it is usually a good idea to start with the business case that was developed to justify the project. Of course, the audience for the Case for Change is not interested in all the gory details like cost/benefit analysis, return on investment, net present value, and so on. However, if you have a well-drafted business case, you can usually glean many of the answers to the questions posed earlier, at least enough to provide the draft for the business people or Working Committee.

In most cases, it is far better to come in with a draft document that people can react to. Many project teams that tried to start with a blank sheet of paper ended the exercise in a real disaster. It led to nit-picking and was rarely successful. Even when you start with a well-drafted document, you will have plenty of heated discussions just trying to edit it!

When Rob Thompson began to construct his Case for Change, he consulted, as suggested, the business case that was developed. It provided him with several of the issues that had prompted the executive team to sanction the project. He also visited with the software vendor who had been selected to provide the Customer Relationship Management software to understand more about how the system would look to the users in various departments. For these visits, he also brought along Paul Ryan, his lead business analyst, because he wanted to make sure he was not overlooking something. Paul provided Rod with an assessment, which concluded that the biggest impact on the organization would be felt by the sales and marketing people. It became obvious to Rod that he would require a real focus on those people if the project would succeed. As a result, for the meeting with vendor related to the expected benefits, he also invited his communication lead, Anne Garcia, to attend to pick up the "selling points" she might need to include in various communications.

After all this preparatory work, Rod felt he was ready to sit down and craft a draft Case for Change. Rod then took the draft to his champion, Paula Dahlberg, for review and suggestions.

Let's take a look at the Case for Change that was presented to the Working Committee for Project Renewal, the Customer Relationship Management (CRM) implementation.

Paula arranged for the Case for Change to be reviewed by Lise Ramsay, even though Lise was traveling. Rod and Paula had a conference call and used a real-time meeting software so they could make changes to the draft together while they were all on the line. That saved the time of having the draft make the circuitous route from one person to the next as each added ideas. By the time the meeting was finished, both Lise and Paula were satisfied that the Case for Change was ready to share with the Working Committee.

Case for Change for Project Renewal	
Question	*Answer*
Why are we doing the current Customer Relationship Management Project Renewal?	The current system, our CTS, does not: • Support a modern medical equipment and manufacturing operation. • Provide just-in-time manufacturing and delivery logistics essential for effective manufacturing and high customer satisfaction.
If we do not do this project, we cannot:	• Respond to our customers' orders effectively. • Schedule the manufacturing of medical products in the quantity required by our customers. • Reduce the amount of inventory we need to keep on hand to handle rush orders. • Reduce rework by accounting and accounts receivable handling credits. • Diminish the number of returns caused by the shipping of the wrong items to customers.

(continued)

Question	Answer
What are the benefits?	The new CRM application that Project Renewal will deliver will allow us and the company to: • Track our inventory in real-time. • Real-time inventory will change instantly with the "auto refresh" turned on. • For transportation and rush orders, allow account representatives to know immediately what products we have on hand. • Present summary and drill-down views on customer information. • Allow us to do what-if scenarios prior to entering an order to maximize discounts and promotions. • Easily enter orders with less paperwork and hassle. • Track our daily and monthly customer orders for more effective and successful projections of customer requirements. • Improve productivity. • Keep up with the dynamically changing industry and eliminate many spreadsheets and duplicate entry steps. • Make quicker decisions based on better knowledge management of our inventory and product mix in a volatile market. • Provide a tool to more accurately and efficiently pinpoint the value drivers within our product lines. • Provide more reliable tool that won't "crash" as often as CRT does.
What if we don't change?	• Our current order entry system will be expensive and difficult to support in the future, and we will be left with outdated technology where the: ◦ Performance of the system cannot be improved.

(*continued*)

Question	Answer
	• The system will gradually become less and less maintainable.
	• We will spend too much time on administrative tasks.
	• We won't be able to take full advantage of new product, business, or market opportunities.
	• We won't be able to efficiently capture the value and potential of our most profitable customers.
	• We won't be able to efficiently model the future requirements of our business.
	• We won't be able to efficiently pinpoint customer value drivers.
	• We will continue to use our individual spreadsheets as our primary order entry tool, which puts us even further behind our competitors.
	• We won't have a central repository for all of our customer data and buying habits.

What do we need to do differently?	We need to
	• Use the CRM tool as primary tool for order entry and customer data and use our personal spreadsheets as a secondary tools.
	• Use the quick deal entry templates with a customized Sales Management Desktop.
	• Use on-demand Sales and Marketing desktop analysis tools.
	• Have sales representatives input most orders including:
	  ◦ Standard orders
	  ◦ Customized orders
	  ◦ Odd-lot orders
	• Utilize the comprehensive audit trails.
	• Develop and follow consistent processes, procedures, and policies.

The Results Can Be Dramatic

Hopefully, you can see the power of providing your end users, particularly the sales and marketing people, with the answers to these questions. Immediately, Rod began to develop real interest in Project Renewal. The reaction of Gary Stiles, the sales manager on the Working Committee, was interesting. He said to Rod, "If you can deliver this project with these benefits, my guys will love it!" Instead of approaching the deliverables of the project reluctantly, Rod was building an expectation and an excitement around the possibilities and potential of the project. As he expected, Rod received a great response from the sales and marketing people. While some of them were still reluctant due to earlier projects that had failed to deliver, most were as excited as Gary Stiles had been.

If you deliver (and hopefully you will!) your project as advertised and communicate using a well-crafted Case for Change, by the time you are ready to roll out the final product, the people who would normally be your biggest problem group will be actually begging you to deliver! They will start driving you to deliver it faster, and you might need to slow them down. Wouldn't that be a change?

Key Points to Remember

- Building a good Case for Change answers the basic question, "Why are we doing this?"
- It also addresses the reasons for the final users to not only accept but also support the deliverables of the project and establishes what will change in clear language for the business audience.
- The Case for Change explains the consequences of failure.

Once the high-level view is articulated through the Case for Change, the hard part begins. Now the project team will need to dig into the details and be able to communicate exactly how things will be better when the project is finished.

Chapter 7

Analyzing Changes
to Business Process

M uch of the reluctance that people within a company feel about these kinds of initiatives is the sense that the project is happening TO them rather than WITH them. They feel like victims with little or no control over something that is very significant to their job. And that generally will scare a person, which is not unreasonable. However, there is a great way to address that feeling, and it ties in beautifully with the communications.

One way to handle the victim mentality is to engage the business and get its assistance in analyzing the business process changes that will occur after the project is delivered. As Rod learned when he started the course of action, at first, the impact was not apparent to the company's leaders. However, as they began to complete an analysis of what would really change once the CRM was installed, they saw some of the significant changes. And as usually happens in these situations, there were key decisions that needed to be made. Rod understood that the key to success was involving the enterprise in these decisions. His decision to involve the various company people in the analysis fostered much more cooperation and buy-in from the users who would ultimately employ the new system. It had the added benefit of allowing Rod to communicate to the entire organization how much everyone really was participating in this project.

Rod decided to avoid one of the common mistakes he had seen companies make: to focus attention on mapping or documenting the current way of doing work. The reason Rod chose not to go in that direction was a real concern—using up valuable time he didn't have! The reality was that those same documents or maps were going to be trashed as the project finally finished, so he did not see the point. The time lag used in creating such materials can cause the project to lose momentum and visibility to the key stakeholders. He thought a better place to focus the energy of the project team and key stakeholders was on the problems or issues that have created the need for Project Renewal in the first place.

> One of the great myths in business today is that technology will solve bad business practices.

When Rod began to work the project plan, he asked Paul Ryan, his lead business analyst, to facilitate a series of meetings with key stakeholders to capture their issues and problems. He specifically asked Paul to focus on the business processes in capturing information from customers and delivering products and services and not on the new Customer Relationship Management technology (Figure 7.1).

> **Definition**
> A **business process** is a collection of interrelated tasks that accomplish a particular goal.

By communicating to them in advance that the focus was on the issues related to business practices, the key stakeholders in Paul's session accepted the fact they did not require any technical knowledge of the CRM. This will also allow them to focus on the "best" way to do the work efficiently and achieve customer satisfaction.

Paul then guided the project team to use the business analysts to compare the different alternatives for handling issues related to customers and match them with the functionality of the CRM. The

Scoring method: Use the scoring method to assess the problems with current order entry problems	Score 0 = none, negligible impact, or an essentially unresolvable Score 1 = impact on efficiency Score 2 = impact on manufacturing Score 3 = impact on manufacturing *and* efficiency
Where the customer has multiple contracts with us, the incorrect legal entity is entered into the order	3
Credit check was not completed before entering the order into the system	1
Based on an incorrect understanding of inventory, a rush order required changing the production schedule	2

FIGURE 7.1   Issues scoring worksheet: Example.

result would be a first pass at possible changes. Rod deliberately chose business analysts who were knowledgeable about MedTech's business. They had also been trained by the vendor to be familiar with the Customer Relationship Management (CRM) software.

> **Definition**
> A **business analyst** or **"BA"** is responsible for analyzing the business needs of clients to help identify business problems and propose solutions.

They were instructed to consider how MedTech's operations would be impacted by the introduction of the CRM and match that with the issues that had been captured during Paul's sessions with key stakeholders.

As the business analysts within the project team explored the CRM and the problems identified, they could begin to understand which concerns the CRM could address and those that cannot be addressed. Anne Garcia, the communications specialist, then took the information and determined how to best present this information to the Working Committee.

> The entire goal of this part of the analysis is to set the right expectations in the minds of the key stakeholders about what problems and issues the CRM can address and those that are out of scope, for whatever reason.

Now the Working Committee began its work on the process changes (see Figure 7.2). Based on the analysis of the business analysts, the Committee assessed the possible alternatives for the way that the CRM will support various business processes presented by the business analysts from Paul's team. Rod communicated very clearly to them that they needed to produce recommendations to the project team and provide direction about the best way to handle the modifications. What Rod had done was put this business-centric group in charge of making the associated decisions.

One of the key elements of the analysis involved the Working Committee's soliciting opinions and concerns from the groups they represented. In other words, Leeland Olson, the member of the committee who was the Controller, would invite others in the accounting and financial areas of the company to provide him with input and feedback on the options the Working Committee was considering.

For example, one of the key changes related to the way customers could be identified in the new system would potentially reduce a great deal of manual work. In the old business process, the accounting department had to manually review an order and determine which contract from that customer applied. The project team had presented different options for the Working Committee to consider.

1. The BAs suggested having the sales representative, who took the order, match the order to the customer contract when the deal was entered into the system. However, the feedback the committee received pointed out they were simply moving a manual process from the back end to the front end, but with little real labor-saving value.
2. Another option was to distinguish the customers with multiple contracts by location since the contracts were generally tied to locations.

Since sales, contracts, accounting, and manufacturing were all interested in solving this problem, all the committee members had

Process Change	
Description of the magnitude of the process change.	
Who will be most affected by the change? (How will they be helped or hurt? If we assume they will be hurt, how will they be hurt? If we assume they will be helped, how will they be helped?)	
Is it feasible to make the suggested changes to the process within MedTech by end of Project Renewal?	
How do you weigh the benefits of the change against the time and effort?	
Plan (What steps are needed to implement this change in your area? What constraints are there? Are there any other initiatives that impact this process change?)	
Test (How should the team test the change to make sure we don't have any unintended consequences?)	
Communications (What do people need to know? When? Who should provide the information?)	
Training (What must people be able *to do* after training is completed related to this change?)	
Leadership (Who would be responsible for this change within the business after the project is finished? What support will we need from them to succeed?)	
Measures (What are some measures of success we can apply to this business process?)	
Any other impacts?	
Process change	
Description of the magnitude of the process change.	

FIGURE 7.2   Template for process change impact analysis.

to poll their constituents about these and other options. Then each of the members came back to the next meeting and reported on how his or her people felt about the modifications.

During the course of the evaluations, Rod discovered through a relationship he had developed with another sales manager that Gary Stiles had not solicited any input from him on a recent process change decision. Before he jumped to any conclusions, Rod decided to check with several other sales managers to see if they have been asked for input—and they had not! At that point Rod took two steps to address the sit-

> Without the ability to explain and elaborate, and to make it relevant to the team, the leader can add no value and is reduced to denying any responsibility for the communication, staying in with the team by denouncing the information more vehemently than they have done.[1]

uation. First, he and Paula Dahlberg, the champion, had a meeting with Gary to discuss how he had circumvented the ground rules established as part of his role as a Working Committee member. Paula received a promise from Gary that it would not happen again. The second was to see if the decision that had been made without input or feedback was critical to the project work. Paul Ryan, the lead business analyst, believed that it was not significant, and the project team did not need to reopen that decision. However, if Paul had reached a different decision, Rod would have asked the Working Committee to reconsider the decision, even if it would be embarrassing for Gary. Figure 7.3 outlines a basic process for decision making.

The beauty of Rod's approach was that the Working Committee now "owned" the decisions and was in charge of handling the changes, making the decisions, and then directing the project team on the agreed-on approach. It was not the project team "imposing" its will on the organization. When it came time to communicate with the organization about how Project Renewal would trans-

---

[1]Bill Quirke, *Communicating Corporate Change* (New York: McGraw-Hill, 1996), p. 222.

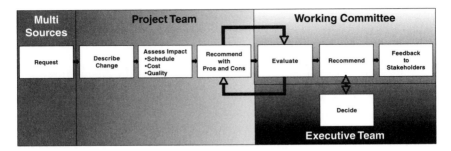

FIGURE 7.3   Process for decision making within the Working Committee.

form the company, it would be the Working Committee who came to support and defend the various changes.

Finally, the Working Committee needed to communicate back to the organization regarding the decisions that had been made. Rod knew he would need to help members with that communication, but the Working Committee needed to deliver it. They were the people who were representing the various functions within the project, and they were the ones who needed to deliver the messages to the company.

Rod asked Anne Garcia to work with key Working Committee members and Paula Dahlberg, the champion, to draft and refine the messages. Paula then brought the communications to the Working Committee meetings and asked for, and received, consensus from each member of the Committee that he or she would all deliver the communications to their constituents and support those communications in any follow-up discussions.

Rod and Paula realized that the quickest way to build uncertainty and resistance within the organization would be if one of the Working Committee members was seen as either disapproving a decision or not fully supporting it. Therefore, the consensus exercise and the agreement were critical before any communications related to process alterations were sent to the organization.

Next, Rod and Anne began to analyze how to communicate and distribute the information on the process changes being made by the Working Committee based on the analysis of options provided by the project team. Typically, there are three ways to address modifications to tasks:

1. Create a communication specifically related to a change.
2. Build the change in business process into the training plan.
3. Build the change in business process into the leadership plan.

Communicating a Change

When the time was right to begin the process of communicating process changes to the organization, one of the first decisions caused Rod and Anne to return to the Common Elements (from Chapter 5). First, they had to determine the right power base for delivering any communication related to a particular alteration. If the modification required a persuasive message because either it would be possible for individuals to ignore the variation and/or it would be difficult to police, they needed to find someone who could credibly deliver the message. If the adjustment required compliance because it was non-negotiable for individuals to ignore, then the message needed to come from a position of authority. Once they had made that decision on "who," they had to determine the purpose of the message (e.g., obedience) and which form of media would be the best way to deliver it. At times there was only a single communication about a single decision regarding a business process modification. Other times it would be important for people to remember message, so the plan needed to include multiple communications on the same message (remember the Rule of Frequency!). Rod and Anne decided to follow up certain communications related to process transformations by developing a communication for members of the Working Committee to use with their stakeholders. They had learned that these types of scripts are particularly important when the change impacts one group in particular. Also, it allowed them to carefully control the communications to the business. And the Working Committee members generally appreciated the help because often they would have had difficulty in articulating the messages effectively. They generally recognized that the memos provided to them by Rod and Anne were better than anything they could have produced. And if they did object to something that Rod and Anne had inserted into the message, Rod and Anne had important feedback on the way they were crafting the communication pieces for their stakeholders.

Building Changes into the Training Plan

Sometimes it will be better to build the information and communication related to business process changes into the training that the operations people will receive before the project deliverables are moved into day-to-day operations. Before you make that kind of decision, make sure the business agrees with the approach.

In considering whether placing the business process change into the training plan, it is useful to think of training as divided into two distinct components: functional training and competency training.

- Functional training: The training normally considered as part of software training that would be provided by the vendor during the installation. Generally, this training focuses on the functions and features of the software product and essentially teaches users how to navigate around and between screens within the software.
- Competency training: The training that focuses on how to use the software within the workflow of the process that has changed. The focus here is to teach users how to use the software to do the work they are required to complete as part of their job.

Very often project managers take a superficial look at training and ask the question, "What will people need to *know* to make the project work?" A different approach would suggest that executing the training plan should focus instead on this question: "What will people need to *be able to do* to make the project successful?" Focusing on *doing* rather than *knowing* is a critical difference. It changes the paradigm from a learning solution to a job-related solution. Basically, people *do* work and hence the focus on doing rather than knowing.

In developing the support for the business processes as part of Project Renewal, Rod Thompson decided that many of the changes would best be incorporated into the training plan. He had Steve Benson, the training specialist, work closely with Paul Ryan, the lead business analyst, to put as much of the process change material as possible within the training program. During the planning phase, Paul and Steve had to figure out how they would capture the information to be inserted into the training. Steve then would work with the seller who provided the CRM application to build the competency training into the standard training the dealer provided. Steve learned the vendor generally only provided the functional training, so Steve would need to develop much of the training materials related to the process changes.

As a quality assurance element, Rod directed Steve and Paul to work with the various Working Committee members to make sure they were comfortable with both the approach to the training, but also the content. Rod wanted to make sure the Working Committee had blessed the training before it was ever delivered to the end users of the CRM.

Steve also learned more about the CRM and decided the best way to handle it would be to develop short modules related to different transactions within the CRM. Modules are defined as short courses of study that, combined, form a larger training program. He then worked with members of the Working Committee, who were also familiar with the software now, to determine which modules would be appropriate for people within various functional groups. That way the training would be tailored and targeted to each set of people, and the process changes would be appropriate for their needs. They wouldn't be forced to sit through hours of training that had no relevance to them. Because they were busy people, he knew the business people would appreciate that approach.

Finally, Steve realized that people would also need to know how to find the help they needed when they forgot or if the Customer Relationship Management software did not behave as they expected after the training was completed. Therefore, he developed a relationship with the information technology help desk manager to understand how the ongoing support would work after the project was completed. He and the manager developed a very specific set of steps for assistance when anyone required it. He made it a priority to build that information into the training so people could find the help they needed.

Building a Leadership Plan

A key element was to communicate how various process changes would impact the company and secure a commitment for company's leaders to support the new CRM. Rod and Paula Dahlberg, the champion, developed a plan for rolling out the business process changes to the middle management people. These were the people who supervise most of the work, so getting their buy-in was critical. As part of the plan, Rod and Paula asked senior managers to participate in management commitment sessions with the managers who reported to them. The management commitment sessions would first of all demonstrate the new software package being used by MedTech. They realized that managers would be much more likely to attend a demonstration than a policy discussion. As part of the demo, the Working Committee member leading the session would highlight the business process changes. The idea was to have the senior managers, along with the appropriate Working Committee members, reinforce the priority placed on implementing these modifications effectively. And the final portion of the management commitment sessions would be an explicit request for the support of these middle-level managers with a commitment from them to use the CRM from Project Renewal properly.

Developing Preliminary Performance Measures

The last element in communicating changes in business processes will be to develop preliminary performance measures. Remember back to Chapter 1: Linking Projects to Business Strategy? An important linkage would be performance measures to provide proof that the improved business performance envisioned by the strategy was really happening. There did not need to be dozens of them necessarily, but Paula and Rod appreciated that there must be an easy way for people in the business to link the improved performance with the project.

Rod Thompson understood the concept and worked with members of the Working Committee to develop a first pass at performance measures for Project Renewal. He and the Working Committee looked at the Case for Change (from Chapter 6) and some examples they came up with for Project Renewal to illustrate the changes that the CRM system would impact as shown in Figure 7.4.

Rod and the Working Committee were now relating Project Renewal to specific performance improvements for MedTech. When Anne Garcia began to develop some communications around the business process alterations wrought by Project Renewal, these were

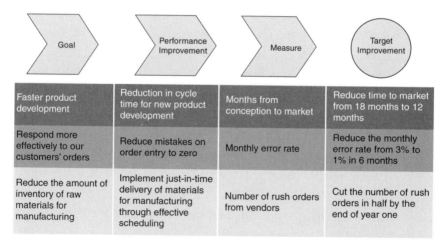

Goal	Performance Improvement	Measure	Target Improvement
Faster product development	Reduction in cycle time for new product development	Months from conception to market	Reduce time to market from 18 months to 12 months
Respond more effectively to our customers' orders	Reduce mistakes on order entry to zero	Monthly error rate	Reduce the monthly error rate from 3% to 1% in 6 months
Reduce the amount of inventory of raw materials for manufacturing	Implement just-in-time delivery of materials for manufacturing through effective scheduling	Number of rush orders from vendors	Cut the number of rush orders in half by the end of year one

FIGURE 7.4   Performance measures for business process changes.

specific examples of how the project would improve the performance of the company.

Key Points to Remember

- Analyzing changes to business processes provides input to both the training plan and the leadership plan.
- Create specific, targeted communications related to alterations in business processes.
- Create performance measures that encompass the modifications.

All of this is working to gain support for the work of the project. In the next chapter, we will look at how to plan a strong foundation through communications.

Chapter 8

Developing Support for the New Business Processes

No matter how successfully the project manager prepares the leadership and the users within the company, there needs to be recognition that backsliding (the tendency all people have to revert to the old way of working) will almost always occur at some point. Even if you have provided the leadership team, especially the sponsor and the champion, with their scripts for the support the project will need, the tendency of senior managers to forget about the project and move on is inevitable. So the question should not be, "Why did this happen?" Instead, the important question is, "What do I do about it?" Answering that question, and the role that communications plays in the answer, is the focus of this chapter.

Addressing the Fairness Factor

It will also include building a wider network of subject matter experts that can not only act as a sounding board for reinforcing the critical changes, but also provide the reality check that alterations were not made in an arbitrary way, but in a methodical and fair way to satisfy the greatest number of people. There will also be a suggested ground rule for decisions that are made to maintain support for the variations in business processes related to the project.

When Leaders Backslide

Rod faced the problem when his sponsor, Lise Ramsay, began to miss update sessions with Paula Dahlberg, the champion. It was reasonable to believe that occasionally there might be conflicts within the schedule that would cause Lise to miss an update session. However, Rod began to see a pattern of cancelling meetings at the last moment, usually the day before or the morning of the regularly scheduled meeting with Paula.

Rod recognized that this pattern might lead to further difficulties if he did not address it quickly and effectively. He recognized the potential to backslide by senior management, so he didn't allow it to make him frustrated. His first step was to arrange a session with Paula to raise his concerns. Paula, as you can imagine, was reluctant to appear to criticize her boss, but acknowledged Rod's concern. Together, they reviewed the format they were using to present information to Lise to see if that could be the source of the problem. After a review, they concluded the information seemed to fit requirements that Lise had provided when the project was kicked off. Then they looked at the frequency of the meetings to see if that might be the source of Lise's reluctance to meet. They concluded that perhaps they could alter the schedule to every two weeks instead of every week. And they concluded they would try to limit the meeting to 20 minutes. The briefing would only be highlights, issues or problems, or items where they needed Lise's help; otherwise, the weekly written report would be sufficient to cover the standard items such as schedule and budget.

Rod and Paula then pulled together an email. In it they made a request to Lise stating that the goal of the next status session would be to determine how to update Lise on the project going forward.

A week later, they had the meeting where Lise stated that she had become convinced the project seemed to be going fine and did not feel a weekly update was necessary any longer. Rod had anticipated this response and worked with Paula on the answer in advance. They agreed to change the timing of the meetings to every two weeks. However, Rod was convinced that they might need Lise's involvement during the last two months before of the completion of the project. So Paula was ready and then asked Lise to resume the weekly meetings in the last two months of Project Renewal. Lise readily agreed. They also agreed on the format of the status report that Rod and Paula would provide Lise between sessions. Rod's fear was that another key stakeholder might ask Lise a question that she would not be aware of or prepared to answer. His experience was that those types of questions are not the detailed questions that users of the CRM might ask, but more directional or of a policy nature. For example, Lise might be asked by the Vice President

> Sometimes the leadership on the project becomes convinced its involvement is no longer needed. You must be prepared to deal with that and prepare a response. In most cases, this situation probably belongs on your risk register where you keep all the other potential risks to your project, but other experienced project managers may disagree. Your company's track record for major project implementations should guide your conclusion.

of Sales, Nick Winters, about the requirement for sales representatives to enter the orders directly into the Customer Relationship Management system. Lise would need to know the recommendation for the requirement that came from the Working Committee after review by a working group. Lise could then, as part of her script as sponsor, ask Nick if he had any concerns about the requirement to test what he had heard. If there were concerns or misinformation, Lise could alert Paula and Rod so they could address the issue and provide Nick with the correct information.

When Other Key People Backslide

Another common situation can occur—members of the Working Committee stop attending the meetings. Remember, the members of the Working Committee were chosen to represent their functional group (their constituency) within the company. In Chapter 7: Analyzing Changes to Business Process, you saw how important the Working Committee members are to the overall communication and acceptance of the project deliverables.

> Today, identification is critically important to organizations for several reasons. First, it acts as a glue that binds employees together in support of the overarching goals and mission of a business enterprise.
> *Peter L. Brill and Richard Worth*[1]

Having a key member of the Working Committee starting to miss meetings without any warning is a potential danger to your project, and you will have to deal with it quickly. Having said that, I realize that the people who are likely to be chosen to represent their group on the Working Committee are probably the same people who are also chosen for other key initiatives within the organization, causing conflicting priorities at times. Other times, it will be other situations. One of the most effective ways to keep the members of the Working Committee focused on the project is to work with the executive leadership team, through the sponsor, to make a successful project a key measure on the personal performance contract of those individuals who have been selected. If they fail to support the project, or the project fails to deliver, their personal year-end bonus would be adversely impacted—and that approach was the one that MedTech took with Project Renewal.

Rod began to get concerned that Gary Stiles, the sales manager on the Working Committee, began to miss meetings. Rod didn't get the feeling that it was another initiative, since the CRM was very

---

[1] Peter L. Brill and Richard Worth, *The Four Levers of Corporate Change* (New York: AMACOM, 1997), p. 139.

important to the sales and marketing groups within MedTech. His first step in addressing the concern was to ask Paula Dahlberg, as champion, to have a conversation with Gary to see if she could uncover the reasons for the absences. Paula agreed to have the meeting; she and Gary had a candid discussion about Project Renewal and Gary's role as the representative for the sales team. It turns out that Gary was involved in quite a sizable sales opportunity for one of the largest healthcare organizations within the United States and Canada. He believed that his Run the Business responsibilities outweighed his responsibilities to the Working Committee for Project Renewal—not to mention that there could be a sizable bonus for him personally if MedTech made the sale.

Paula reported back to Rod, and they decided this was one of those situations where they needed Lise, as the sponsor, to intervene. Paula arranged a conference call through Lise's assistant since she would be traveling extensively for several weeks.

The two of them provided Lise with the background on the dilemma facing them if a key member of the Working Committee continued to miss meetings. The obvious alternatives they discussed were to either (1) replace Gary with another sales manager or (2) realign Gary's priorities to allow him to refocus on Project Renewal. The obvious complication in this case was that Gary did not report to Lise, so she couldn't work to direct his priorities. However, at the conclusion of the meeting, Lise promised to make a phone call to Gary's boss, Nick Winters, and discuss how to handle Gary's commitments to the business for both the Working Committee and to the financial well-being of the business.

Lise came back the following week and reported to Paula that she and Nick had worked out a solution to the problem, and Gary would be back to regularly attending the Working Committee meetings. The details of the solution were not revealed to either Paula or Rod, but they really didn't need to know—they had what they needed for the project to be successful—a fully participating member of the Working Committee.

I hope you can see through this scenario how as project manager communication between the sponsor and champion can help you prevent the erosion of support from key managers within the business. As project manager, you will very rarely have the personal leverage to address a situation like Rod faced with Gary. Keeping key stakeholders aligned is one of the key responsibilities of the senior management team. And they must be counted on to fulfill that responsibility. Most senior managers are quite willing to support the project when they understand how they can support it and when.

Urgency and Decisions

There will also be an element of urgency for decisions from senior management and the Working Committee. Early on, the project manager must clearly understand the balance between speed and need for decisions related to the project. In Figure 8.1, the speed and urgency of the need can determine the type of decision a project manager needs from the management team.

On the other hand, a project manager must understand the politics that go on inside the executive suite and not expect a senior manager to make a decision beyond his or her span of control.

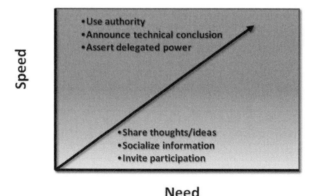

FIGURE 8.1 Urgency of decisions. As you can see from the figure, the faster a decision is required, or the higher the need, the more a different decision model might be required.

If other departments or functions are directly impacted, it will be incumbent on the project manager to either

1. Develop all the evidence and materials for the senior manager to have conversations with his or her peers, or
2. The project manager will develop the same materials, but will be the person responsible for delivering that message and requesting a decision.

Either way, we are talking about time. To reiterate, if Rod Thompson was asking Lise Ramsay to make a decision quickly because time was critical to the decision, he must make that crystal clear at the outset. Also, he must alert Lise that if the decision was delayed for whatever reason, the impact on schedule and budget must be included in the information so Lise and the other senior managers at MedTech can make a business decision. For business reasons, the management team at MedTech was, in certain circumstances, willing to sacrifice some time on the schedule because they were not prepared to use their unilateral authority to make a decision about some aspect related to the implementation of the CRM from Project Renewal.

Key Points to Remember

- The temptation for reverting to the old way of doing things can be overcome by communications.
- Use subject matter experts to assist your communications for the new direction.
- Alter the engagement for senior leaders if necessary, but don't allow them to "check out."
- Assist key Working Committee members in managing their priorities as required to keep them involved.
- Always let leaders know when a decisions are time critical.

Now that we have seen the importance of support from all parts of the company, let's move to the next chapter and look at the actual tasks that you will need to include in your plan.

Chapter 9

Developing an Operations Integration Plan

If you are clear about the initiative and the relationship to the performance improvement from Chapter 1: Linking Projects and Strategy, you come to the enviable conclusion that all undertakings cause changes within the day-to-day operations of the business. There is a basic truth that we, as project managers, must come to grips with if our assignments are to be a business success—people are very reluctant to change. If you want evidence, just think of all the people you know who are overweight or have high cholesterol and should be watching their diets and avoiding certain foods, but don't. Just think of all the individuals you know who are smokers despite the overwhelming evidence that it can kill them. All of these situations call for a change in basic behavior, but the old behavior persists. When your deliverables are introduced to the day-to-day operations, you will need to overcome that instinct to continue with the old behavior, and communications are critical to success.

Some programs create big changes, like Project Renewal at MedTech, and others are smaller in scope. The one thing they have

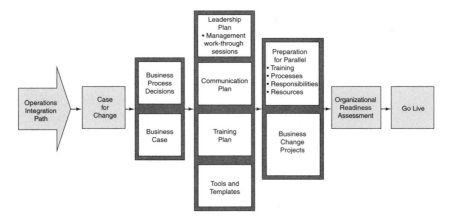

FIGURE 9.1 Operations integration model.

in common is the need to integrate the finished product into the operations of the business. However, many project managers don't always recognize that with transformation comes resistance. Again, much of the business value of many ventures is lost because the project manager did not understand how to use the same rigor in developing the operations integration plan (Figure 9.1) to motivate different behavior within operations as he or she did in developing the work breakdown structure, budget, and schedule.

If you look at Figure 9.2 for the likely employee response to changes, the situation can look bleak, since over one-half of the peo-

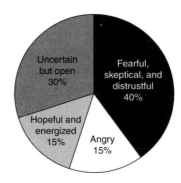

FIGURE 9.2 Employee response to threat of change.
Source: Data from Roger D'Aprix, *Communicating for Change* (New York: Jossey-Bass Publishers, 1996).

ple will not respond positively to modifications the finished project will require.

However, in this chapter, we will explore an operations integration framework for building a plan to successfully implement the project deliverables into operations. For the purposes of this book, I am using "operations" as a generic term to mean day-to-day work within the business. Communication is an essential part of any plan associated with operations integration during a project.

Five conditions for ensuring the successful incorporation of the finished project are the foundation for our look at project communications. The five requirements to effectively assimilate project deliverables are to communicate:

1. A Case for Change.
2. Understanding of the business process changes once the project is delivered and the issues addressed.
3. Available support from the project team to assist operations in using the project deliverables.
4. Preparation, including training, the project team will deliver to make sure everyone is prepared for project deliverables.
5. Timetable for when various changes will happen so no one will be surprised.

Let's look at each requirement and see how this type of communication can prepare the operations people for the completed project.

Case for Change

We already looked at the important Case for Change in Chapter 6: Writing the Case for Change (it might be useful to return to that chapter and review the Case for Change for Project Renewal). One important additional idea here is to use a step-by-step maneuver for translating and communicating the Case for Change. To illustrate the point, let's look at how Rod Thompson approached it with Project Renewal.

In the early stages, Rod developed a draft document with Anne Garcia and other members of the project team as illustrated in Chapter 6. He then briefed the Working Committee and asked them to preview the Case for Change with their constituents and report the reactions they had. The advantage of Rod's approach is twofold:

1. The members of the Working Committee can "translate" the content within the Case for Change into words that their constituents can identify with.
2. The Working Committee will be able to provide the project team with feedback on the types of questions and opinions people had to the project during their discussions.

Both of these are important advantages in helping to prepare various functional groups as you work to deliver the project and plan additional activities to address any questions or concerns raised during this early stage of communication.

Later on in Chapter 17: Preparing Operations to Accept the Deliverables, I will give you some additional ideas that are appropriate for the Execute phase of the project. Here we are only talking about planning for operations integration.

Understanding the Process Changes

During the course of the project, there will be several alterations in the way the business will function during its day-to-day work. For example, Project Renewal will change the way

- Sales representatives enter customer orders.
- Manufacturing schedules production of products.
- Warehouse tracks inventory and delivery.
- Marketing mines customer data for future marketing programs.
- Credit manages customer accounts and credit limits.
- Accounts payable handles billing and invoicing.

These are just some of the high-level examples of process changes introduced by the project. There will be a multitude of detailed changes investigated by the Working Committee during its work (see Chapter 7: Analyzing Changes to Business Process). All these revisions must be communicated to the business. At this point, the idea is to develop a plan for delivering that information.

Rod Thompson developed a plan to provide a specific communication to the Working Committee every two weeks during the Execute phase of the project. He asked Anne Garcia to plan on providing specific written pieces for each segment of the business as the variations in processes became apparent. Also, he planned on having a "Frequently Asked Questions" section on an internal website for later reference for any key stakeholders. Rod also made sure that Steve Benson, his training specialist, was developing the training plan to include business process modifications into the training that was being developed as preparation for the CRM users.

Support Provided

During the course of the project, it will become apparent that various job aids will be helpful to assist people as they cope with adaptations in processes. It will be important to plan for that. Rod Thompson, our MedTech project manager, had put 40 hours in his project plan for his training specialist, Steve Benson, to devote to building a variety of tools and templates for the enterprise in addition to the time he has designated for training (which will be explained in more detail in Chapter 10: Developing the Communications for the Project). Rod also needed to plan for the introduction of the various tools to aid stakeholders if their indoctrination needs to occur outside the training session. For example, he held off on some tools because there were minor changes in screens right up to the implementation. In that case, he planned on holding off on any tools that showed screen shots until right before the system went live. In that case, he needed to work with Steve Benson on a plan for distributing those tools or templates in preparation for the users of the CRM modules, and he communicated that approach.

He also had allocated time within the plan for Anne Garcia to prepare various communication documents to explain the use of the job aids that Steve had developed and to let various key stakeholders know the tools and templates were coming (both during training and after as required).

In addition to the time to build tools and templates, Rod built time into his project plan to allow his business analysts to collaborate with the Working Committee members on creating standard operating procedures (SOP) documentation for capturing the new ways of working. These records would be important for maintaining consistency and sustainability within MedTech after Project Renewal was completed. He recognized the documentation was also very useful as a training tool for new people who would join MedTech after the project was finished. And finally, Rod built in time on the plan with Paula Dahlberg, the champion, for developing a process to keep the SOP documentation up to date after the project was completed.

Preparation for Project Deliverables

The most obvious preparation the stakeholders will need is training. We will look at training in more detail in Chapter 10: Developing the Communications for the Project, but it is important as a key requirement for implementing successful operations integration. However, there are other elements that must be planned for. One is the performance expectations for the users by their supervisors after the project is implemented.

For example, in our case study of Project Renewal, Rod built time into the plan for Lise Ramsay, Paula Dahlberg, and the appropriate members of the Working Committee to meet with various groups of managers and supervisors. The purpose of the meetings was to gain their support. It would be important for managers to hold their people accountable for using the CRM properly and to accept the new responsibilities related to the CRM. Again, as an example of one meeting, Lise Ramsay, Paula Dahlberg, and Gary Stiles met with sales managers regarding how the roles and responsibilities of sales representatives would change when the CRM went live and how sales managers would need to hold those reps accountable for inputting the correct information into the CRM.

Finally, to build excitement for the new system, and to communicate how the CRM would work, Rod scheduled a series of sessions he called Demo Days. These sessions were held at various locations over the lunch hour. The plan was that a member of the project team (usually a business analyst) and a member of the Working Committee led the session. They developed a quick, 20-minute demonstration of the system with time added to handle questions from the audience. They decided to advertise the sessions through posters and emails. And they would contact various managers and supervisors to encourage them and their direct reports to attend. When these sessions finally happened during the Execute phase, they were a big success and created real excitement about the new program.

Understanding the Timetable

The timetable is essentially a subset of the project schedule that highlights various key milestones. Key stakeholders do not need all the details of the schedule; they only need those portions that affect them directly.

Rod worked with members of the Working Committee to stage the timing of various key milestones of the project. Therefore, he needed to build that time into his project plan as well as how he would communicate the stages to a broader audience.

This was a very important element. Communicating the timetable required that Rod keep his project plan up-to-date and revise it continually so he could keep this important communication element updated. He realized that an out-of-date project schedule could lead to faulty timing in important communications to key stakeholders.

Requirement	Requirement	Requirement	Requirement	Requirement	Result
Case for Change	Understanding the Process Changes	Support Provided	Preparation for Project Deliverables	Understanding the Timetable	Operations ready to receive the deliverables
	Understanding the Process Changes	Support Provided	Preparation for Project Deliverables	Understanding the Timetable	Confusion; lack of interest
Case for Change		Support Provided	Preparation for Project Deliverables	Understanding the Timetable	Old ways of work continue
Case for Change	Understanding the Process Changes		Preparation for Project Deliverables	Understanding the Timetable	Frustration, anger, and disappointment
Case for Change	Understanding the Process Changes	Support Provided		Understanding the Timetable	Disregard for the deliverables and lack of motivation
Case for Change	Understanding the Process Changes	Support Provided	Preparation for Project Deliverables		Wasted effort and lack of orderly progress

FIGURE 9.3 Missing requirements model.

In Figure 9.3, when all five of the operations integration requirements are in place, the result is the successful integration of the project deliverables into operations. In each of the subsequent lines, there is an assumption that there is only one missing requirement and that all the other requirements have been satisfied. Unfortunately, the result of missing any particular requirement is in the right-hand column. As you can see from Figure 9.3, it is very important to complete all the requirements successfully. If you do a fine job on all but one of them, the project will end up with a situation where the integration of the project deliverables will be incomplete.

Napoleon's Thirds

When you think about communicating with people, it is good to remember the lessons of history. It is well known that Napoleon employed a strategy to win over his generals when he wanted to embark on a new campaign. Napoleon realized that within his leadership team (the generals) he would face men who would divide into roughly three camps. One faction were loyal and trusting and would follow him anywhere. All he needed to do was give the orders, and they were ready. The second group was just the opposite. They would be against almost any suggestions and immediately tell Napoleon why it was a bad idea. Finally, the third bloc were those generals who were uncertain, but would listen to the emperor's proposal and make their decision based on the merits of the campaign and the approach for overcoming the risks. In attempting to win over the generals so he could embark on his campaign, who do you think Napoleon focused on? The third group, of course. He knew that he already had the first group, and he was unlikely to sway the second camp no matter how hard he tried. His strategy was to focus on the third group because if he got them to agree to the campaign, he now had two-thirds of his generals committed. This forced the second group into a position where they had little choice but to follow along. This strategy became known as Napoleon's thirds.

In working to communicate and gain commitment from the operations unit, recognize that you will probably find the biggest resistance to the modifications your project will deliver within the ranks of the middle managers. The problem for you in delivering the business value of your project is that this group supervises most of the people who actually do the work. Having them buy into the value your initiative delivers is critical to its success. So one of the key tasks during the planning phase is to conduct an assessment of the management team, particularly the middle management ranks affected, and attempt to identify which of the three camps they will fall into. It will help you to focus your attention and communications in the right places.

Rod Thompson, our project manager, and Anne Garcia, the communications specialist, used the Napoleon's thirds strategy to peg the management team of MedTech into Napoleon's three factions. Anne and Rod planned to create unique communication pieces for each group—not so different that they would react to the difference, but based on where they were related to the camps and the changes the project deliverables would create.

For the first group (on board from the beginning), the communications were very upbeat and took on an almost "cheerleader" quality to keep enthusiasm high. For the second group, the communications were kept informative and factual in their tone. There was no attempt to persuade them on anything related to Project Renewal. For the third group, the communications would be factual, but would include a perspective from a respected technical leader within the organization (this aspect will be covered much more in Chapter 10: Developing the Communications for the Project). This meant Rod had to build in time and activities into the project plan not only for him and Anne Garcia, but also for some of the managers. They would need to prepare communications and/or develop agendas for management meetings to address some of the key alterations being wrought by Project Renewal.

Key Points to Remember

- Start building for operations integration with the Case for Change.
- Ensure there is an understanding of the nature of the process changes.
- Provide people with support to ease frustration during the transition.
- Prepare and communicate the timetable so people know when things begin to happen.

In summary, then, as project managers, we must prepare for delivering our project deliverables to operations. We must take as much care in planning for the transitions as we did in building our work breakdown structure, our schedule, and our budget. If we do take the same care, we will face a group of users at the end who are ready, willing, and able to use our project deliverables. The result of being prepared will be a project that succeeds in meeting its business goals and targets—not only a technical success, but a business success as well. And it is built on a foundation of strong communications—the subject of the next chapter!

Chapter 10

Developing
the Communications
for the Project

The Basics of Communications: It's All About Perceptions

Much of our understanding comes from our perceptions. Every time you communicate with people, your project team, stakeholders, or anyone else, you must keep their perspective in mind. Figure 10.1 illustrates how perspectives influence people's understanding. Before you communicate anything to anyone, analyze your audience. Ask yourself the following questions:

- What information do people need?
- Does the message I'm sending communicate a particular feeling or attitude? (You may need to alter the tone depending on how you answer the question.)
- What is the best medium for delivering the information?
- Who is the best person to deliver the information?
- How should I deliver the message?

- When should people receive the information?
- How will I receive feedback on how people react to the information?

In a recent project, Rod Thompson had learned a tough lesson from a type of situation that all project managers find themselves in at one time or another. The project was coming into the final months. Things had gone very well up to that point, but the final few months threatened to undo all the goodwill that had been built up over the previous 12 months. While many of the issues that surrounded the project were more complex than is necessary

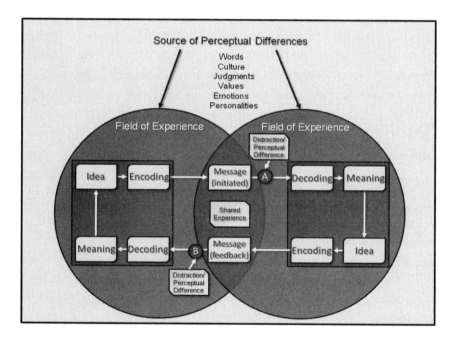

FIGURE 10.1   A basic communication model demonstrates that our perception comes from our experiences, culture, word choice, values, and judgments. We use all these elements to encode and decode messages, and communication only occurs when the circles overlap. Otherwise, misunderstandings are inevitable.

Source: Vijay Verma, *Human Resource Skills for the Project Manager* (San Francisco, CA: Project Management Institute, 1996). Reprinted with permission.

to detail here, there was a basic flaw in Rod's communication strategy. He had fallen into the habit of communicating with the business through email only. As most of us know, between the tremendous amount of email (much of it unnecessary) coupled with spam, many people will ignore email after a while. And that is what happened to this project. Rod recovered from that nearly fatal flaw, and this time decided to bring a communications specialist to help him build a new and more robust communications plan for Project Renewal. That is why Anne Garcia joined the team.

What Does a Communication Plan Look Like?

Building a communication plan is critical to the success of any project. It is the most common way of letting the end users of the project know what will happen to them and when. We'll look at several components of the communication plan in greater detail:

- Stakeholder analysis
- Sensitivity analysis
- Information needs
- Media requirements
- Delivery personnel and power bases
- Timing requirements
- Common definitions
- Feedback loops
- Macro and micro barriers
- Jargon and acronyms

Stakeholder Analysis

Some stakeholders will have more interest in a project than others. In the case of a project to develop a new customer information database for the company, sales and marketing management are probably much more interested in this project than others in the manufacturing facility, but all of them have an interest! The purpose of doing a stakeholder analysis is to see if we can determine how they will be concerned. These examples illustrate the point from the stakeholder analysis that Rod Thompson and Anne Garcia did for Project Renewal:

- **Sales** is concerned about how the information will help sell more products and services to existing customers and if it can help land the business of some prospects that are not currently customers.
- **Marketing** is concerned with getting information that will help identify buying trends that may be the result of marketing literature. Marketing people will also hope to see trends that will indicate the types of new products customers are likely to buy in the future.
- **Research and Development** takes the information that Marketing provides and works to develop products that will meet the new demands and can be manufactured at a price that will produce a profit.
- **Manufacturing** is interested in the order entry so it can plan production schedules in a way that will ensure enough products are on hand for sale, but not too much that will require storage in a warehouse.
- **Purchasing** wants the system to feed information into its financial systems to be able to track purchases to make sure customers are not exceeding their credit limits as well as provide information to track their payment records.
- **Management** wants visibility into the buying patterns of customers so managers can make rational decisions about where to invest limited capital and human resources that will allow the company to continue growing.

Sensitivity Analysis

All these groups have some unique interests the project manager will need to reflect upon when developing the communications plan. For example, sales professionals will be sensitive to any system that seems to add a layer of bureaucracy to the tough business of selling goods and services. They will rightly complain and follow with a statement something like "What would you rather I do, sit around all day entering information into a computer or be out on the street selling products?" The answer to that question is obvious, but the project team that does not take that into account will run into some serious resistance later on as it tries to implement the new customer database.

The management team and all others will have different concerns, but the way the team addresses them will be just as important during the course of the project.

Information Needs

Different groups need different types of information. Rod Thompson and Anne Garcia understood that salespeople would be much more concerned about how information was entered into and taken out of the system since they will be the ones most likely asked to do that. And they were at the front end of the value chain. Marketing people would be much more interested in the reporting capabilities, and the accounting people would be more concerned about accuracy of the information for invoicing and payments. Accounting would want to know how much and what type of information can be extracted from the system, but would be bored by the level of detail the salespeople need on order entry. Likewise, each stakeholder group will have its own unique information needs. Rod and Anne worked hard to build each type of information requirement into the Project Renewal communications plan (an example is provided later in this chapter).

Media Requirements

Rod and Anne contemplated carefully about how, exactly, they were going to deliver information to each of the stakeholders. When referring to media requirements, it means the vehicle or channel

Let me reiterate a basic point that has hurt hundreds of projects over the years: Sending out email messages is not communicating! While email can be one component of the overall plan, Rod really needed to make it a minor medium as he had learned from that earlier effort.

Rod and/or Anne would use to deliver the information required by each of the stakeholders. They wanted to deliver the facts in such a way that they have the best chance of success and so that people would actually pay attention to the information!

Instead, Rod and Anne considered a variety of other delivery mechanisms, such as:

- Town hall meetings
- Presentations
- Staff meetings
- Desk drops
- Wall charts
- Web portals

Figure 10.2 illustrates the various types of communications commonly used, and the check marks indicate the situations where it is generally most effective.

Type of communication	Group	Individual	Written	Spoken	Formal	Informal
Email		✓	✓			✓
Reports		✓	✓		✓	
Meetings	✓			✓		✓
Presentations	✓		✓	✓		
Teleconference	✓			✓	✓	
Town hall meeting	✓			✓	✓	
Telephone		✓		✓		✓

FIGURE 10.2 Types of communications and their characteristics for certain situations.

Delivery Personnel and Power Bases

Consider who would be the right person to deliver the message. That will depend on thinking through the power base that is required to complete that message successfully. As you can see in Figure 10.2, different sources of power will give different results. For example, you'll notice that the most persuasive power base is expertise. As a communications expert, Anne knows that if Project Renewal needed a message delivered where the desired outcome was to persuade people, she would need to have that message delivered by someone who was considered an expert (whether internal or external) by the people being targeted for the message. If the message signaled that a change was mandatory and was not negotiable after the project was completed, that message must be delivered by an executive or senior manager for that stakeholder group. The best rule, then, is to pick the source that matches the result you want.

> One caveat to executives delivering a message about a mandatory change—people must believe the change will be enforced. If the business has a poor record for enforcement, the project manager is likely to get a poor outcome, which means you might actually be worse off than if you hadn't communicated at all!

As you can see from Figure 10.3, what you need to accomplish determines the power base you come from and the purpose of the communication. How would Project Renewal apply that to the CRM implementation?

One critical area that Rod discovered through his business analysts was a shift in the way sales reps keep track of their information on existing customers. He considered having a leader such as the Vice President of Sales, Nick Winters, send the communication on the way the customer information must be maintained in the future—and that would be a reasonable idea. However, another strategy he discerned from the power base was to use one of members of the sales staff as a communicator. That is ultimately how Rod and Anne decided to handle this particular situation.

They decided that the project team would provide one of the real "stars" of the sales department (someone recognized by the

Power Base	Desired Outcome	Actual Results
Expertise	Persuasion	Strong, particularly related to details or in technical areas
Admiration	Voluntary compliance	Strong, but not everyone will have the same level of admiration, so compliance may be spotty
Reward	Motivation	Different people are motivated by different rewards, so unless the reward is tailored almost to the individual level, the outcome is highly variable
Position of authority	Mandatory compliance	This power base will only produce results if the business believes management will enforce compliance
Coercion	Compliance through fear of consequences	Usually creates significant resistance and sometimes even sabotage

FIGURE 10.3   How the power base affects certain outcomes.

entire sales staff as a very successful representative) a demonstration (or prototype) of the new CRM tool and ask for his or her suggestions on how it could enhance the ability to generate sales. After preparing a slick demonstration in cooperation with the vendor, Rod and Anne asked the sales rep to speak to her colleagues on the benefits she saw. Project Renewal saw a huge difference in the response of the sales team. In fact, the difference was so dramatic that Nick Winters stopped by later to thank both Rod and Anne! He had been very reluctant to antagonize his sales staff over this issue, but he was willing to do it if required. He was grateful that Rod and Anne had found another way to motivate the sales representatives. He realized that his sales team would really listen to one of their peers because she was respected as an expert, not by position (like he was as the Vice President of Sales), but by performance, the test that really counts for salespeople.

Timing Requirements

The right timing for the message is important. If you provide information too early, people may ask questions you can't fully answer just yet! They may want more details than you can give them, particularly early in the project. If you wait too long to relay information, then the project is moving forward at a pace that will not allow people who are impacted to keep up, and they may feel like you are making decisions without them. While you don't really need their consent, timing your information correctly will make them feel like you are seeking, and receiving, their approval. It will really provide excellent buy-in from the ultimate customers!

Common Definitions

Often certain industries, or even companies within an industry, will have a unique, set language—MedTech certainly did. It was important that Rod, as project manager, made sure any contractors or consultants he hired to work on Project Renewal knew the unique definitions and jargon used within the company. To make sure he was prepared, he asked Anne Garcia to interview internal subject matter experts (such as the Working Committee) and develop a glossary of terms and jargon used within MedTech. She prepared a "dictionary" and put it on the project website so external people could reference it easily until they learned the lingo.

> Make sure all the key people on your team are familiar with the common definitions associated with your project.

Feedback Loops

In any communication plan, there will need to be a feedback loop to assess how the information has been received. Occasionally, there can be unanticipated misinterpretations or other consequences based on communications that were not understood they way they were intended. Stepping back for a moment, it makes sense. Making sure everyone involved understands common definitions is one way to prevent those misunderstandings from occurring. However, different interpretations of the information can lead people to different conclusions than had been anticipated. Therefore, the only way to know for sure that the communication was understood correctly is to have a feedback loop.

The way Rod decided to build a feedback loop within Project Renewal was to develop a relationship with some key people within various stakeholder groups and contact them after a certain key communication had gone out. He also asked his key team leaders, Paul Ryan (business analyst), Joshua Larsen (technical lead), and Luke Johnson (IT liaison) to develop a similar relationship with key people within their areas of responsibility within the business. They were all seeking the same information: what the reaction was to the message and what people said around the water cooler. That helped Rod and Anne determine if various communications were successful or if they needed to refine or even modify the message next time.

Another benefit of a feedback loop is that it lets you know what rumors are circulating about your project. Address those rumors as quickly and fully as possible. Nothing will build the credibility of your project more than having a message delivered about a rumor that only started a few hours or days ago. The stakeholders will believe you are listening to them, and this will reduce their anxiety about your project considerably.

Macro and Micro Barriers

As you build your communications plan, think about macro and micro barriers. Some of these barriers are obvious, others are not so obvious, but all are important to consider and plan for to be effective.

Macro barriers are those large barriers that prevent effective communication. One such barrier would be simple geography. If the potential customers are scattered over multiple locations, obviously the ability to communicate is more difficult. You will need to consider how to handle the situation and overcome the barrier. Another macro barrier would be different languages; different nationalities and culture will be a major consideration as you plan your communications. Getting a project team member from each language, nation, or cultural group to assist in the communications will be critical to success.

Micro barriers are much more subtle. One obvious example would be attitudes that people, as a group, have about the ultimate goals or success of a project. Maybe a similar project was attempted several years ago and was a complete flop! Now everyone thinks the business concept is flawed and will never succeed. Other similar micro barriers may surround the project and will need to be considered as you figure out how you will communicate to people.

Jargon and Acronyms

When you communicate, use only jargon and acronyms that are used by the stakeholders of your communication plan. For various functional groups, it is easy to slip into using jargon and acronyms that are common or popular with that function, but are not familiar to others. A simple example of an acronym might be the use of AMA. If you were talking to a group of business people, they would probably assume you were referring to the American Management Association. However, if you were speaking to doctors, they would assume you were referring to the American Medical Association.

Developing Effective Messages

Communicating on a project is an art as well as a science. The better you get at it, the smoother your project will flow from beginning to end. You must provide enough information to keep team members informed without boring them. Every word counts. What you send, to whom you send it, and when you send it are always issues. If in doubt about a message, always wait. When you decide you need to say something, however, these guidelines should help you decide exactly what you want to say (regardless of the medium you choose). Also see Figure 10.4 for a sample communication plan.

Stakeholder	Sensitivities	Info Needs	Media	Who Delivers?	Timing	Feedback	Richness	Purpose	Power Base	Barriers?	Definitions, Acronyms, etc
Sponsor - Lise Ramsay	Very busy and not interested in the details	Progress against budget and schedule	One-on-one meetings	Paula Dahlberg	Weekly	In meetings	Very rich—personal	Generally only variances	Authority	Schedule	Careful not to use IT acronyms or other unfamiliar jargon
Working Committee Chair - Paula Dahlberg	Difficulty in balancing various personalities and responsibilities	Issues - both technical and organizational Potential delays in schedule	One-on-one meetings	Rod Thompson	As they occur	Immediate	Very rich—personal	Work to prepare either the sponsor or the executive team if a problem has occurred	Expertise	Conflicting priorities	Careful not to use IT acronyms or other unfamiliar jargon
Working Committee Members	Narrow view based on their function and its needs; multiple priorities with conflicting priorities	Options with enough detail to allow them to assess pros and cons and make recommencations	Meetings called as needed—range from meetings to emails depending on the size of the problem or the risk involved	WC Chair with the support of the Project Manager	As needed	WC Chair needs to check within the functions if SMEs are seeking input from their colleagues	Can receive most information in writing, except bad news	Get them involved so they will advocate the solutions within their functional teams	Expertise	Cross-functional needs are different	Keep the language oriented to the business not IT

FIGURE 10.4 Sample communication plan.

- Always draft the message and then carefully edit it before you send it. This will help you be more concise in the message and ensure that you have covered all the required points.
- Think about the audience's expectations, any actions required as a result of the message, and your expectations after the message is delivered.
- Justify your choice of delivery medium for the message and the timing of it.
- Clarify the purpose. Start the message with an introduction that identifies the issue, context, or opportunity of interest.
- Make any required actions clear and specific in the message.
- Be as concise as possible without seeming insensitive or rude.
- Never surprise someone with information, particularly if it is bad news. For example, if you will be discussing a problem during a meeting, make sure the right people know what you will say before they get there.

If you use the same rigor and discipline in planning your communications as you do for developing the work breakdown structure, schedule, and budget, you will be amazed at the results. People will comment on how well informed they feel and how comfortable they are with the project.

Key Points to Remember

- Carefully consider your stakeholders.
- Understand that they will all have certain sensitivities.
- Consider the information they need and how to deliver it to them.
- Factor in the timing of communications.
- Manage all barriers to communications.
- Be on guard against jargon, acronyms, and lack of common definitions.

Another of the important documents you will develop using the tips and techniques from this chapter will be the Project Plan Memorandum. This document goes to the management team and explains exactly how you have planned to deliver business benefits. That's what we'll cover in the next chapter.

Chapter 11

Writing the Project Plan Memorandum for the Executive Team

In this chapter, I want to move back to a written form of communication that is crucial to successful project completion. After all, the overall plan is what the you and the team members will be implementing to provide the final results expected from the business executives. Communicating the effort that has gone into the detailed planning phase of the initiative is culminated with the Project Plan plus the accompanying Memorandum to the executive team (referred to in Chapter 2: Preparing the Leadership).

For the purposes of this chapter, I will focus on the important communication aspects of the Project Plan Memorandum (referred to as the memo). Many of these elements, such as the review of the business case, are often neglected at this phase when moving into the Execute phase. Finally, this chapter will focus on specific tips and suggestions for writing a memo such as an executive summary.

The key stakeholders within the leadership must approve the plan, since they are the ones who will guide the project and give it the correct business direction. The memo should include

- Revised Business Case: A description of the reasons for the project and a justification for sanctioning it based on the estimated costs, expected business benefits and/or savings, and an identification of the risks.
- Schedule: The work plan showing the order in which tasks are to be carried out and the time allocated to those tasks.
- Budget: The total amount of money allocated or required to accomplish the work within the timeframe outlined in the schedule.
- Resources: The people and equipment assigned to the project from both inside and outside the company.
- Final Scope Definition: A definition of the total products and/or services to be provided by the project plus those elements that are not included.
- Work Breakdown Structure: The grouping of project results or outcomes that must be produced during the project where each descending level represents increasingly detailed descriptions of the work.
- Subsidiary Management Plans: Supplemental plans that serve to support the overall management of the project plan.

They need all this information in order to approve the project. And as the project manager, Rod Thompson needed their agreement to ensure project support for Project Renewal as he moved into Execute phase.

Review of the Common Elements for All Communications

In developing the memo for Project Renewal, Rod Thompson, our project manager, went back to the common elements for all communications covered in Chapter 5: Common Elements for All Communications. Here was how Rod analyzed those common elements.

Audience Analysis

Rod knew that the primary audience for the memo would be the members of the executive team. These were primarily the senior managers within MedTech who had a stake in the outcome of Project Renewal. Rod also realized these executives were very busy and would not be likely to dive into the details except where it impacted their area of responsibilities. Therefore, Rod decided he would develop the Project Plan Memorandum like an executive summary. The executive summary approach would allow him to capture the high-level information that all of them would be interested in.

Rod also realized there may be additional secondary readers who are not part of the executive team, such as members of the leadership team, who may also read the high-level memo but not the detailed project planning document. Therefore, he had to be sensitive to any concerns they might have about the project.

Purpose

While the rationale is fairly obvious in the case of Project Renewal, Rod decided that his purpose really went beyond a simple point like "accept the project plan and sanction the team to move forward." Rod decided he wanted to build enthusiasm within the leadership team, so that became his purpose—not just acceptance of the project plan, but real enthusiasm for the results Project Renewal might bring to MedTech.

Strategy

Rod thought long and hard about the strategy he would use. He considered big picture/small picture because he wanted to show how Project Renewal fit into the corporate strategy of MedTech. He also considered compare/contrast because there had been a project the year before that had left a bad taste in people's mouths because the communication was so poor during the project. He did not want his project tainted by the experience people had with that project, and he wanted to differentiate Project Renewal. However, he finally settled on problem/solution because he felt the management team was really interested in how Project Renewal and the Customer Relationship Management system could solve the problems MedTech had been having over the last several years.

> Based on the analysis Rod did, he really could have chosen any of the approaches for developing the Project Plan Memorandum. The importance was not the specific strategy that he chose, but that he thought about it and believed the line of attack he chose would help him achieve the purpose of his communication—to build enthusiasm within the executive team.

In Rod's mind, these problems had finally caused enough pain to motivate the management team to do something about it.

Formal Versus Informal

Rod realized this memorandum was an important document to his project and required him to be quite formal in the way he both wrote it and presented it.

Oral Versus Written Communications

In this case, Rod knew he would be both producing a set of documents and making a presentation (see Chapter 13: Presenting to Stakeholders During Project Execution for more details). Therefore, Rod enlisted the help of Anne Garcia, his communications specialist, to help him produce sharp, professional-looking documents and slides. He was not going to look anything but polished in front of this group of executives.

Others Were Not Required

After reviewing all the common elements, Rod concluded he had covered all that affected him at this point in time. He did not need to consider elements like power base or barriers because he did not see any relevance. As a final quality step, Rod decided he would review his analysis with Anne Garcia and Paul Ryan, the lead business analyst, to test whether they agreed with his assessment. They provided him with some feedback, and he incorporated those suggestions into the first draft.

There is one other important element to the review—the business case for the project—to make sure the initiative is still viable to address the business needs outlined in Chapter One: Linking Projects and Strategy. Rod asked Paul Ryan and Joshua Larsen, his technical team lead, to carefully review their estimates for costs and schedule. He wanted to run the numbers again to make sure he had a business case that made sense and a plan he could comfortably recommend moving into the Execute phase.

Writing the Project Plan Memorandum

During his audience analysis, Rod had determined that writing an executive summary would be appropriate since most of the management team would not be interested in delving into all the details. Therefore, he asked for help from Anne Garcia to help him write the executive summary effectively in addition to providing all the detailed information in the project plan. In reviewing his thoughts with Anne, she suggested the following ideas for developing an executive summary.

Purpose of the Memorandum

In general, a Project Plan Memorandum is an abstraction of the key points of a larger planning decision support package that describes to management the planning for the project and the readiness of the team to execute the venture. Although an executive summary may frequently involve the same process, the memo's primary purpose is to apprise or inform the executive team of a plans for the project, risks that have been identified, issues that have been uncovered that the project team will need to address, and opportunities that have surfaced during the course of planning. Consequently, the memo summary may be used with a larger document (the one it summarizes), or it may stand alone as the only documentation that summarizes a project.

Strategy for the Memorandum

The Project Plan Memorandum, like an executive summary, requires excellent organization. However, the Project Plan Memorandum needs to be the epitome of logic. The logic must be obvious from the first word to the last word of the memo. The visual organization (i.e., the white space, format) should complement the logical organization. Visual organization techniques that are particularly suited to the memo include well-thought-out power headings and bullets. Good project summaries usually contain a message within the message. That is, the headings, if they were all that was read, will provide a primary meaning; the remainder of the summary would highlight the main points, conclusions, and recommendations that support the primary communication.

After completing the analysis and reviewing all the deliverables he would need as support materials, Rod began to develop the memorandum itself. Anne referred Rod to a guidebook she had received while attending a training class on business writing. He used many of the tips from the book to develop the memo using the construction of an executive summary.

Anne guided Rod in developing the first draft of his memo by suggesting that he

1. Keep the members of the executive team in mind.
2. Write his first draft as if he were talking to them.

Anne also guided Rod to edit his work after the draft was finished and not try to write and edit at the same time. She suggested that people who try to write and edit at the same time often suffer from writer's block. Rod used her suggestions and came up with a reasonable first draft. Now he was ready to edit the draft.

However, just as he was ready to dive in and start editing, Anne suggested he take a rest. She proposed he move away from the manuscript and if possible, tuck it in a desk drawer for a couple of days. Anne advised that he not turn immediately from writing to editing.

The reason she provided? She indicated to Rod that the brain selectively forgets things for us. By setting the writing aside, he will forget some of the reasons why he wrote sentences and phrases the way he did. If he waits a day or two, he can approach the writing almost as if it were written by someone else. He will be ready to criticize what he wrote and not necessarily defend his own words. She convinced him it was the best way to improve his writing.

She also related another interesting writing tip—something else would happen when he was away from what he had written. His subconscious will continue to work on the ideas. He would find problems solved when he returned to the draft. The improvement to that awkward sentence would be right there on the tip of his tongue. And there, waiting for him, would be the exact word he was searching for when he wrote the draft.

Editing the Memo

Anne reviewed Rod's first draft of the Project Plan Memorandum and gave him some feedback she felt would improve the document. She pointed out to Rod that it is important to remember that the memo is a more personalized communication between a project manager and the members of management. The style of writing, although not entirely informal, was much less formal than a general project decision package that it summarizes. In a general decision package for a project review, MedTech has adopted a formal style that is based upon organizational standards and requirements that are strictly applied when the executive team reviews a project before execute. In general, for these reports, Anne related, the tone should be neutral. In Project Plan Memorandum, the tone always will be positive with subtones that will vary to represent Rod's analysis of the project, the overview of the readiness, and Rod's concern for business impact upon the MedTech organization delivered by Project Renewal.

Because the project plan memo and an executive summary are both a synopsis, they must be efficient. Anne reminded Rod these reviews represent a digest of a larger document, therefore they should not be longer than the document they summarize! On the contrary, the rundown should be very efficient and allow the executive team to move through information quickly and economically.

Writing Style

Anne suggested that Rod follow three specific guidelines when editing his draft:

1. Prefer concrete words to abstract ones.
2. Prefer a single word to a phrase.
3. Prefer short words to long ones.

Anne also reviewed his draft for clichés and jargon to make sure he had not used any. She asked him to check for accuracy for elements such as dates, figures, or personnel. Finally, she suggested Rod use the spell checking feature within the document to identify any potential misspelled words.

Finally, Anne asked Rod to work through the draft and cut out any unnecessary words. She reminded him that short and concise were critical elements in an executive summary document.

Here is his final product.

Executive Summary

The name Project Renewal was chosen for this project because the implementation of a Customer Relationship Management (CRM) system will provide a step-change opportunity for MedTech to have the system required to support a modern medical equipment manufacturing company with growth potential to reach over $1 billion in annual sales within five years.

Problem: The system we have been using for the past seven years (CTS) is outdated and no longer reliable. It does not allow us to effectively schedule the manufacturing of our products, forces us to keep too much inventory on hand, and does not allow our sales representatives to respond very effectively to our customers, particularly when they require either rush deliveries or special orders. We also have far too many customer returns because we delivered the wrong equipment.

Solution: The implementation of the CRM system will allow us to

- Provide just-in-time manufacturing to reduce inventory.
- Improve the speed of delivery of our products to our customers.
- Respond quickly and effectively to our customers' requests for rush orders by allowing sales representatives the ability to access inventory and manufacturing schedules online over the Internet.
- Improve cash flow by reducing accounting errors and the rework created by logistical errors.

Opportunity: By using the CRM effectively after the implementation, MedTech management will be able to

- Make quicker decisions based on better knowledge of the value drivers within our product lines.
- Understand our inventory and product mix during times when the market becomes volatile.
- Create a better view of our customer orders for more effective forward projections of customer orders.

Return on Investment: Based on our planning, the project team calculates the NPV for this project at $14 million over five years after implementation. All the details of the calculations and assumptions are contained in the attached project plan.

Recommendation: The project team would recommend that the executive team approve the overall project plan for Project Renewal. We believe the opportunities are well worth the investment and we also believe we can manage the risks to the project effectively.

In addition to being analytical, the memo as a summary of the project can also advocate direction, such as the recommendation that the project move into the Execute phase. In fact, the Project Plan Memorandum should usually end with next steps or recommended actions.

Key Points to Remember

- Review the common elements for all communications and apply the appropriate ones.
- Write first and then edit—don't try to do both at the same time.
- Use an executive summary to communicate quickly and efficiently to management.

The Project Plan Memorandum is a powerful business writing tool. As a key communication between a project manager and the executive team or sponsor, it provides information that is on target, with a purpose, clearly organized, expressive, and efficient.

Now that we have finished the easy part—the planning—let's look at how communications can be a valuable skill during the execution phase of the project.

Chapter 12

Using Communications
to Handle Risks

A risk is defined as a condition or event that, if it occurs, will have an impact on the outcome of the project. While there are some positive risks, most project managers focus on those with a negative influence.

There are three types of risks most project managers must manage during the course of a project:

1. Technical risks
2. Business risks
3. Organizational risks

These risks usually come in three categories:

1. Known risks
2. Predictable risks
3. Unpredictable risks

When most leaders think of risks to their project, what comes to mind first are technical risks. And leaders usually do a very good job of mitigating those risks because they fall into the categories of known or predictable risks. However, they often fail to consider the two other areas of risk. Business risk and organizational risk are often just as predictable but are usually not assessed or planned for. If these hazards are not considered, they can affect the overall benefits delivered by the project.

Business risk occurs when a project is technically successful, but fails to deliver the economic or other business value that was envisioned when the project was sanctioned. In this chapter, we will examine several potential business risks that you can anticipate and provide ideas for mitigation strategies to reduce the impact or avoid the threat altogether.

Also, it is important to anticipate organizational perils. These dangers occur when the company either actively or passively resists the changes created by the project deliverables. Another consequence may be a reduction of the ultimate business value the project should have realized. This chapter will illustrate common company threats that a project manager might face and provide strategies for mitigation or avoidance.

Any discussion of risk must also consider how manageable these dangers are. Usually, those hazards that have a higher manageability factor require effective communications as part of the mitigation strategy.

In the traditional risk matrix shown in Figure 12.1, most often the items listed are viewed in two dimensions represented by the x and y axes—impact and probability. When using communications as a mitigation strategy for these threats, a better way to think about risks is to view the impact as value × likelihood on the y axis and then manageability on the x axis. For example, Rod identified one key danger as the departure of a key individual from the Working Committee. However, he realized this situation could be managed pretty well to lessen the impact on the project by having a process in place to identify potential replacements for each committee member. However, another issue Rod recognized was the possibility that the vendor delivering a CRM would give him a system that was not fully functional. With this kind of problem, it would be much more difficult to manage the situation because it

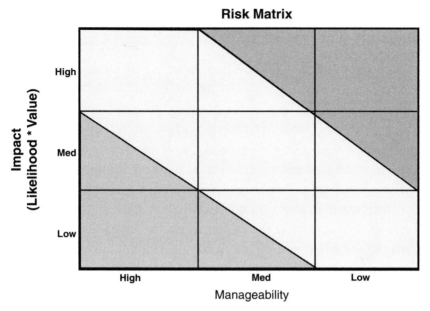

FIGURE 12.1   Risk matrix.

emanates from outside his span of control. The communications to the various stakeholders within MedTech depends as much on the manageability as it does on the potential impact to value and likelihood. In these two cases, Rod communicated differently. For the first, regarding the Working Committee, Rod communicated the need to have a back-up person identified for each function. He framed the request to senior management as the need to cover for committee members when they couldn't make the meetings or they were on vacation. Regarding the tardy vendor, he had a mitigation action in place to identify potential delays and communicate immediately to Paula Dahlberg, his champion, and to Lise Ramsay, his sponsor, through Paula. The purpose of the communication was not only to keep them informed, but to make sure they understood any delays NOT due to issues related to his project team.

> There are risks and costs to a program of action. But they are far less than the long-range risks and costs of comfortable inaction.
> *President John F. Kennedy*

Managing Business Risks Through Communications

In another situation, Rod Thompson faced a difficult state of affairs. He had a status meeting with the project team as usual on Monday morning. During the course of the review, Joshua Larsen, his technical lead, reported there were technical problems occurring in the Singapore location. After the meeting, Rod decided he needed to investigate what was going on in more detail to assure himself that Josh was handling the situation correctly.

Joshua and one of his key technical team members gave Rod a high-level overview of the problem. For an unknown reason (at that time) the CRM system had some performance issues in Singapore. While the technical group was testing different components, the Singapore team noticed the application was running considerably slower in Singapore than in other locations. When Rod asked if the same problem was being experienced by the team in Europe, the technical players reported that the application seemed to behave normally in those European locations where it had been tested.

Rod asked Joshua and his team to prepare a summary for him of the issue—when the problem first appeared and what they were doing to address it. He also wanted an estimate as to how long they could work on it before it would impact the overall schedule (and Rod could use that to estimate the impact on the budget). Rod realized that a significant delay in the rollout of the CRM would badly erode the business value the executive team hoped to achieve when they sanctioned the project.

Rod wanted to brief Paula Dahlberg, the champion, as soon as possible, so Rod asked for the report from the technical team, and he wanted it on his desk by Wednesday afternoon. He chose that time carefully since he wanted to brief Paula before the Working Committee meeting, which would be held as usual on Thursday afternoon.

On Wednesday, Josh provided his report. It had most of what Rod needed. Josh had given Rod a good set of steps he was pursuing to uncover and correct the problem. However, Josh had not given Rod an estimate of time it would take to pursue this course of action and the tipping point where the problem could affect the rollout schedule. He asked Josh to go back and develop those estimates. And he needed that information by the end of the day.

In the meantime, Rod had arranged to meet with Paula at the end of the day on Wednesday to go over the agenda for the Working Committee meeting the next day. He had not talked to Paula yet about the problem, because he did not want to have that conversation until he was armed with the correct information. Joshua and his team provided the estimates to Rod in time for the meeting with Paula, and now he was ready to speak with Paula about the situation.

Joshua and his team provided Rod with the estimates he needed. The ballpark figures revealed that they had 3 weeks to uncover the problem and fix it. If they could not correct the problem within that timeframe, they could keep the project on track by adjusting the rollout schedule. The project team could rollout the project in Singapore last and not impact the overall schedule at all. While Rod appreciated the positive nature of a change in the rollout schedule, the project team had planned on using Singapore as the first location because it was the smallest and its business was the least complicated. Changing to another location would be harder and might be more difficult than Josh was willing to admit. Armed with this information, Rod was now ready to meet with Paula.

> Framing is defined as describing a situation through communicating in such a way as to encourage a certain perception and to discourage others.

In meeting with Paula about this problem, Rod realized that she is a person who, when confronted with a problem, generally is concerned about how others will react to it. Therefore, in anticipation of that concern, Rod had met with Anne Garcia, his communication specialist, to discuss how to best frame the issue first with Paula and then with the Working Committee members.

In framing the issue, Rod had to start the conversation by telling Paula there was a problem, but he and the team had a plan to fix it. He made sure from the beginning of the meeting that Paula would not have to deliver bad news to the management team. Then he went through the performance issue the team had uncovered and, at a high level, how they planned to handle it. Finally, they came to a decision to notify the Working Committee about the problem.

> Anything that begins, "I don't know how to tell you this" is never good news.
> *Ruth Gordon, Academy Award Winning Actress*

Rod's biggest fear was that potential rumors would start. He was well aware that people in Singapore knew about the issue, and he wanted to head off the type of morale-destroying rumors that had plagued the last big initiative within MedTech. Rod and Anne discussed the plan to communicate with the Working Committee, and it mirrored the approach they had taken with Paula. However, Paula decided she would like to briefly discuss the situation with certain key members of the Working Committee in advance of the meeting. The three of them worked through the talking points Paula would use:

1. We know there is a problem, and we have a plan for fixing it.
2. The project team has a timeline and a backup plan to keep the project on schedule if the problem cannot be resolved in Singapore within the allotted time.
3. We will keep you informed on progress, and you will not be in the dark if you are asked a question about the problem.
4. We need your help in letting the project team know if there are any rumors circulating within the company about the problem and what those rumors are if they are circulating.
5. We need your support while we fix this problem properly.

The strategy worked beautifully. The Working Committee appreciated the candor and felt prepared to handle any questions that might come its way. Committee members decided to use the same talking points that Paula had used with them should the issue come to their attention or as a way to answer any questions people within their groups might have.

Managing Organizational Risks Through Communications

One of the business risks Anne Garcia raised during the planning phase of the project centered on the scheduling group within MedTech. Since the old legacy system MedTech had used had very limited functionality for the schedulers, this group had become very adept at using spreadsheets to manage their jobs. They had spreadsheets for managing the scheduling of products, viewing the status of products in inventory, and managing their own work as best they could. Even though they knew the new CRM system could be a great benefit to them, they did not trust the system to provide them with the correct information to do their jobs, and they were very reluctant to give up their spreadsheets.

The problem with the stance the schedulers had taken was the redundancy and inefficiency the company would experience if the schedulers could not be persuaded to abandon their spreadsheets. If the schedulers could not be convinced to change their minds, some of the business value gained through greater efficiency would be lost.

Rod Thompson decided to handle the problems specific to the schedulers by bringing together a working group to address the issue. He worked with Paula Dahlberg to define and communicate the problem and the nature of the recommendation they were seeking to solve this problem. They asked Walter Fisher for input on the three or four people who could handle this working group using two criteria:

1. The people had to be considered some of the best people working in the function by their peers.
2. The individuals would stand by the recommendation they made to the Working Committee if others in the scheduling group questioned their recommendation.

The working group took a few weeks to review the problem and analyzed various options before recommending a phased in approach to implementing the CRM within the scheduling group. They also felt that schedulers would begin to quit using their spreadsheets once they felt more confident in the CRM. When the Working Committee accepted the recommendation, they asked this special group to deliver the message to the schedulers. Anne Garcia worked with the three people selected to solve the problem to provide them with the key talking points they would use to explain the problem and the recommended solution. They used the Change Impact Assessment (from Chapter 7: Analyzing Changes to Business Process) as the way to organize the information and to demonstrate to the scheduling community the process the working group had used to arrive at the recommendation.

Based on the analysis done by the select group and the targeted communications delivered, the schedulers accepted the recommendation and felt like their legitimate concerns had been heard and addressed. This group realized this project team had really listened to their concerns (unlike their experience with earlier projects), and while it was not the perfect solution in their minds, it was certainly acceptable. You can see part of Rod's risk matrix in Figure 12.2.

Managing Risks Through Communications

Risks will always occur during the course of a project. Many of those occurrences will never arise, and the planning will remain just that—planning. However, a smart project manager will use communications as part of the strategy for managing risks when they do occur. Often people will help in creating the solution if they are aware of a problem. An overview of the risk management process is shown in Figure 12.3.

Instructions:
1. Consider technical risks (e.g., data used by the CRM may not be accurate), organizational risks (e.g., a change required by the CRM will be rejected by sales), and business risks (e.g., the assumption for cross-selling in the business case may be too high)
2. Assess each risk for both impact and probability
3. Draw the risk tolerance line (see example below) that is acceptable
4. Develop risk management plans for all risks that are identified above the risk tolerance line

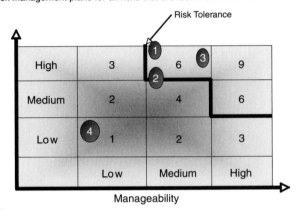

5. Complete the risk matrix below as part of the planning process

Risk Description	Who controls?	Impact	Probability	Exposure	Mitigation Plan
1. Organizational Risk– Other initiatives cause a loss of key people for the project	Paula Dahlberg	3	2	6	Communicate regularly to key managers who have people working on the project and explain the importance of the contribution made by their people
2. Technical Risk – CRM doesn't produce quality data to replace the current system	Project Renewal Team: Paul Ryan Joshua Larsen	3	2	6	Step 1 – Set up conference room trials and run over xmas period to obtain data for review and analysis. Step 2 - Working Committee members (SMEs) work together to analyze and improve output.
3. Technical Risk – Project Execution requires too much effort by departmental people in the time available	Project Renewal Team	3	2	6	Front End Load (FEL) key process activities early in project execution plan. Schedule to ensure the best utilization of departmental people.
4. Business Risk – Authorized Resellers won't sign off for proposed workflow changes	Project Renewal Team Paula Dahlberg	3	1	3	No action required at this time. Monitor for change in status.

FIGURE 12.2   Risk analysis and planning tool.

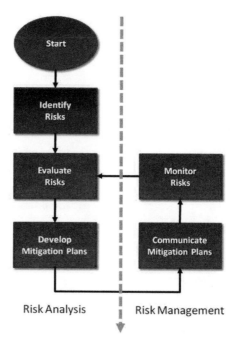

FIGURE 12.3   Risk management process.

Key Points to Remember

- Never surprise stakeholders with a risk—keep them informed as events unfold.
- Be sure to frame the situation correctly so you influence the way the stakeholder responds.
- Stay positive, if possible.
- Have a plan for mitigating the issues, particularly those that are highly manageable.

In conclusion, effective communications can be very helpful in managing those events and situations that can threaten to derail your project.

Now we move to one of the hardest types of communication for many project managers—giving a presentation to stakeholders.

Chapter 13

Presenting to Stakeholders During Project Execution

The fear of getting up and talking to others hurts the careers of many project managers because, as the *Harvard Business Review* reports, the number one criterion for advancement and promotion for professionals is their ability to *communicate effectively*. Clearly, making a successful presentation, whether to your Steering Committee, your boss, or other stakeholders, may play a major role in your career advancement. So how do you do it? While this chapter won't be a complete guide to presentations, you will

> Project stakeholders believe they have a legitimate claim. . . . And a successful project requires that diverse stakeholders work together to accomplish multiple and not always entirely congruent goals, for without their support, the project cannot achieve its goals.
> *David I. Cleland*[1]

---

[1]David I. Cleland, Stakeholder Management, in *Project Management Handbook* (San Francisco, CA: Project Management Institute, 1998), p. 58.

receive some ideas for planning a constructive presentation for any of your stakeholder groups.

In our MedTech case study, Rod Thompson was asked to make a presentation to the Steering Committee on how he planed to prepare the end users to utilize the CRM application. Anne Garcia, our communications expert, guided Rod Thompson through a step-by-step approach for developing his presentation.

Decide Your Purpose

Anne explained to Rod that the first step in preparing a presentation for a stakeholder group was to decide the purpose. According to her, the lack of a clear purpose is one of the two most common mistakes made in a presentation. The listeners are left scratching their heads and thinking "So what am I supposed to do with this information anyway?" Sometimes in a project there is a temptation to think that the project manager is just "giving an update." But more often, the project manager really needs the stakeholders to do something or must persuade them to agree with something. So, for Project Renewal, Rod might define his purpose this way—"The purpose of my presentation is to persuade the executive team that we will prepare our employees adequately for their new jobs after the implementation." That is quite different than "My purpose is to update the executive team on the training we will provide the users."

> The way you organize the information will depend on your purpose, so make sure you clearly determine your purpose.

There are usually five basic objectives that may be chosen for any presentation:

1. Advocating: Convincing or selling a point or approach to the audience (which was Rod's objective).
2. Instruction: Informing or teaching your target audience something about your project.

3. Inspiration: Motivating your audience to act on something related to the project.
4. Stimulation: Stimulating debate or discussion among the stakeholders.
5. Gratification: Entertaining or amusing your audience (highly unusual during a project, but a possible objective nonetheless).

So let's take a look at the basic objectives and see how they might apply to a project.

Advocating

Rod had been asked to present to the sales managers and give them an overview of his project so that they could understand why the company was moving in this direction. Here he was selling the idea to a target stakeholder group who should understand the benefits a CRM will offer them and their account representatives. This stakeholder group will be key to the project's success, so building the presentation around this objective helps them to provide their own "sales" support later on.

Instruction

Rod had been asked to give an overview of the project to the executive committee of the company so they can understand what the project was all about. He would probably choose instruction as his basic purpose. He would want them to know the schedule and business outcomes of the project as a bare minimum. However, he might also cover the business case for the project and the overall goals.

Inspiration

Rod had been asked to brief the same executive committee, but in this situation the need was to make sure they would provide the support for the project that would be critical for its success. In this case, he would choose inspiration as his basic purpose. Rod wanted to motivate them to assist him in getting the entire organization behind the project, because he was concerned that he would meet stiff resistance at times. Providing information that convinced the executive team to back him with their departments would be a key to a successful presentation.

Stimulation

In this case, Rod had been asked to make a presentation to the Working Group. He wanted them to consider possible alternatives to order entry forms (to be completed online) so that the right information could be captured during the deal entry for later use by several departments. Obviously, the presentation needed to stimulate discussion and get them involved in the solution. The outcome he desired was to create a situation where the final result came from the business itself, not as a dictate from the project team.

Remember, if you don't know what you have in mind, how is the stakeholder group supposed to figure it out?

Let's take a moment to review the high points from Chapter 5: Common Elements for All Communications.

Analyze the Audience (Stakeholders)

As Rod Thompson prepares for a presentation, he needs to realize that different stakeholders create a need for him to alter his information so he can meet their needs. For example, he would present very different material to the management team than he would to the end users of the CRM. They have different needs for information and different understandings about the project itself. Therefore, the next step was to really think about who he was speaking to and ask himself a series of questions, including some of the following:

- Who are the key people who will attend and influence the others?

- What do they already know about the project?
- Do I know their attitude about my project?
- Do I have the right credibility to speak to this audience or do I need to bring someone along with me who has more or better credibility?
- What concerns or questions will they want addressed or answered during the presentation?
- How do they receive information? For example, do they prefer a lot of facts and data, or will they be more interested in how it will affect them?
- Do I know enough about this group's level of commitment?
- Who is likely to dislike my ideas or information and what will they dislike?
- Who loses power or access to power if my project is implemented successfully?

The answers to these questions are critical to being properly prepared to present to any stakeholder group. To help answer the questions, and make sure you do a "sanity check," I would encourage you to get a coach within the stakeholder group who will be able to tell you how people in that group will respond and react to your information. You need a coach who is on your side, but who will also provide you with the unvarnished truth.

Let's look at our case study and see who the stakeholders might be. Some of them become obvious right away:

- Account representatives
- Sales managers
- Marketing personnel
- Product development
- Manufacturing

These people were keenly interested in the project because a CRM has direct and immediate impact on the way they do their jobs—and it was obvious to them that it does! They wanted information about how Project Renewal would affect their jobs and performance.

However, there were other stakeholders that Rod needed to consider who had an active interest in the success of the project, but for a different reason.

- Project sponsor
- Executive team

These people were the ones who are "paid" for the project. The project sponsor, Lise Ramsay, was the individual whom the other executives held responsible for the successful implementation of the CRM, including delivering the value outlined in the business case. Depending on the internal politics within the group, they may be willing to actively support the project, but they may also choose to deliberately distance themselves from it. Why? Too often projects do not deliver on the promised value, particularly large projects such as Project Renewal. Executives are very reluctant to be associated with a project that they fear may fail. So getting the executive team behind an initiative can be difficult, and any presentations to motivate them must include a focus on success and reward.

There are other stakeholders who will be impacted by the project but are not as easily recognized as stakeholders. Some of these people are

- Accounting
- Scheduling
- Transportation
- Human Resources

How are they involved? In our case study, here are just a few examples:

- The accounting people would be responsible for producing invoices that will be sent to the customers, and they would depend on the sales office to enter the customer information correctly. They would also need to have data on any special requirements or requests that particular customers ask of them. So they had a definite interest in what happens in this project.

- The scheduling people would be responsible for scheduling the manufacturing and delivery of the products from the company. They would be concerned that they have the orders correctly entered as well as any special instructions for assembling the products and would rely heavily on the data in the system. Otherwise, they feared they may disappoint the customer and undo all the hard work the front office did in selling the products.

- Likewise, Transportation will need to rely on the CRM to give them the shipping instructions for delivery and for data that is correct.

- Finally, Human Resources was concerned on a variety of fronts. For example, the new CRM required new training during new employee orientation. They realized they would be tasked to develop new job descriptions that include the use of the CRM in them. And these are just a few of the examples. You may be able to think of many more.

During any project, and for any presentation, the project manager must be able to address any concerns or objections that the stakeholders may have. Some project managers try to duck the issues, and that usually leads to problems. For example, Rod knew that both Accounting and Scheduling were concerned that the sales reps would not be held accountable for entering information correctly into the CRM. If he tried to duck the questions, or discount their concerns as trivial, these two groups would be not support the project. Why? Because they would feel that their departments would be asked to clean up a lot of the mess made by the sales team within the system. It would look like more work to them, and they would not be thrilled at all. Therefore, even before the presentation, he had a meeting with both Lise Ramsay and Nick Winters, the Vice President of Sales, to discuss accountability for entering data. He asked for, and received, assurances from Nick that sales representatives would be responsible for entering customer information correctly into the CRM. If they did not, he would call them on the carpet and ask for reasons. Now Rod could answer the questions with answers that would reassure these key stakeholders.

As part of preparing the presentation, Anne advised Rod to brainstorm all the questions the stakeholders may have for him and prepare to answer them.

There are also two more or less universal objections stakeholders will have. They usually come down to two basic concerns:

1. The CRM solution provided by Project Renewal will not work.
2. They do not see the need for Project Renewal the way others do.

For example, if the presentation was to Information Technology, there is a good chance people may feel that the current application for entering and tracking customer data is just fine, and they do not understand why the company is making this change in the first place. Rod needed to develop an answer for that concern. He decided he must either cover it during the presentation or have backup materials he can refer to as he fields their questions. Thinking in advance about the situation and the stakeholder group should determine when to address these concerns.

One approach is to just take them head-on during the presentation itself. That was the decision that Rod made in his presentation to the IT group. He gathered the facts and used them to blunt the objections. The other way, obviously, was to simply wait and see if an issue arises and handle it then. However, my experience has been that this may be harder at times because it may look like the project manager was trying to avoid this difficult objection. In either case, he must be prepared with additional information in case it is needed for these objections and that may include handouts or other reference materials.

Likewise, when Rod Thompson gave a presentation to the marketing department on the project, he had to carefully consider the concerns and objections that this department had. As he thinks through their concerns, he realized that one of the key factors that marketing believes drives its success was the ability to watch trends in purchasing and correctly anticipate where customers were going in their buying. Then they develop campaigns designed to highlight that direction and how the company can fill the need. They were very concerned about whether the CRM would give them the data that they have mined very successfully from the old system.

As part of the presentation, Rod also realized he needed to analyze any assumptions he was making as part of his logic. He took some time to also analyze what happens to his logic if the assumptions were changed. Many times, the concerns expressed by people are related to starting with a different set of assumptions. When that happens, a project manager may need to defend his assumptions, or he may need to address issues based on their assumptions as part of the risk planning. What gave the stakeholders more confidence was recognizing that Rod had thought about the issues and had a plan for addressing them.

Our project manager has developed a series of questions that he thinks they would like to ask. He will be prepared to answer those questions during the course of the presentation with as much detail as he has at this time.

Strategy

The other critical success factor in pulling together a successful presentation is to choose a strategy that will match the audience and the purpose you are trying to achieve. If you watch any of the many shows on television about the legal profession, you will often hear the judge ask one of the lawyers, "Where are you going with this, counselor?" Too often listeners are left with the same problem. They are having trouble following the logic of the speaker, and it frustrates them. So what can you do? The best solution is to use one of the common strategies (go back to Chapter 5: Common Elements for All Communications).

As Rod Thompson, our project manager, was building a presentation for the marketing department, so he decided that a **Question/Answer** strategy would fit. He decided that he would address their concerns head-on and give them the confidence that his project would fulfill their demands and more. He decided on that strategy after reviewing the content of his presentation first using a **Problem/Solution** strategy and also a **Big Picture/Small Picture** strategy. And he conferred with his contacts in the marketing department to sound them out on the strategy. They agreed with his assessment that the **Question/Answer** strategy would work well with their group.

The final three thoughts about strategy are these:

1. **Keep it simple.** This does not mean to talk down to the stakeholders, but remember that they cannot go back over it if they miss the point as they can when reading something. So keeping the information simple and practical helps to ensure someone does not get lost along the way.
2. **Keep it in perspective.** That is, their perspective. Always look at what you are saying from the viewpoint of the stakeholders you are talking to by referring back to your audience analysis.
3. **Use handouts carefully.** I usually recommend providing handouts at the end of the presentation. That way, people are not shuffling through the pages and not paying any attention as you speak. However, that is not always practical or possible. Essentially, use the audience analysis to determine when to use handouts and how much additional detail they will need to contain.

Build It in Three Parts

The classic format for presentations suggests dividing a presentation into three distinct parts: the introduction, the body, and the conclusion. Here is a brief outline of each.

- **Introduction.** In the introduction you establish your purpose, cover the benefits people will receive by listening to you, and provide them with a roadmap or quick listing of the topics you will discuss so your listeners can follow along.
- **Body.** Follows the strategy you decided earlier and contains anywhere between three to five main points along with supporting information. It may seem odd to limit the body to only three to five main points, but research has clearly shown that this number comprises the limits of what most people can comprehend while listening. If you want to think about it in a similar context, think about the last time you went to a social gathering and met a number of new people. How many names did you remember? Most of us would only remember a few. As you finish the main points of the body and before you move to the conclusion, ask for questions (see the next section for more details on answering questions).
- **Conclusion.** After you notify your audience that you are finishing, start by recapping your purpose, the main points, and the benefits that you covered during the presentation. Finally, do not forget to thank them for their time and cooperation with the project.

Practice

Finally, practice at least a few times to make sure that your timing and transitions from one part to another are smooth and polished. And practice the presentation out loud. Surprisingly, your presentation will actually sound different when you say it versus how it "sounds" in your head. Also, practicing out loud will help you deliver it effectively and help you to hear if you have too many "ums" and "ahs" while you speak. These are called fillers and can be very distracting if there are too many. You could also practice with a voice recorder and play it back to listen for fillers as well as to hear how you sound to others. Make adjustments based on your assessment of the presentation.

Look in the back of this chapter for Figure 13.1, which contains templates for preparing a presentation. This guide will help you think through the ideas and put them in an order as well as provide an outline of the presentation.

Questions

Often during a presentation, a project manager will be asked a series of questions. My experience has been that some project managers address questions better than others. In researching why that seemed to be true, one critical success factor seemed to be that the project manager recognized that there are different types of questions and each requires a different type of answer. I would suggest that these are fairly typical questions and some suggested approaches for answering them. They are

> The best way to anticipate questions from the audience is to do a thorough audience analysis.

- **Direct Question.** This is the type of question we generally think of. For example, the question is "What can you tell me about changes there will be in the ways invoices will be processed?" This person simply wants direct information.
- **Summary Question.** In this question the person is trying to test whether he or she understands your main points. It might be stated as "So you're saying that this new system will reduce the amount of re-work we must do in accounting?" To answer this type of question, try recapping what you have said and clarify what this person has already heard. The key here is to try to use different words than you used the first time. If you simply repeat the same words, the listener may still be struggling to figure out if she is connecting with your ideas and information.
- **Logic Question.** This person may be trying to use logic to challenge the presenter. It might be something like "You are saying that this system is easier to use but then you are showing

us that there are three more steps for entering information. How can you say that it's easier?" Here, the best answer is usually the experience of the business analysts or other subject matter experts who have used the system. Always back up by data or evidence to support your claim.

- **Experience Question.** This person is trying to use his personal experience to dispute the information you are providing. It might sound something like "I tried what you suggested and it didn't work. How do you explain that?" The best way to counter this type of question is to use the experience of your team, or yourself, and reinforce that for you and your team it worked as advertised. Avoid getting into an argument over their experience—you were not there and you will always lose that argument!

Visual Aids

In developing the visual aids that will help you deliver your message, here are some suggestions that should make them more effective.

> When developing visuals, use the Rule of Six as a guideline for developing slides. The Rule of Six says that you should limit your slides to six bullets per slide and six words per bullet.

1. Most importantly, do not develop any visual aids until after you have covered all the earlier steps described. Visual aids are only developed to enhance the content of the message. Far too often they are developed first, and their appropriateness to the audience has been overlooked. The true test of the visual aids will be if they help you achieve your purpose with the stakeholder group you are talking to.

2. Keep them simple if possible. Slides that are too busy or complicated cause the listeners to work very hard, and many of them simply won't! Also be careful with the colors you use. For example, if the stakeholder group is accounting, don't use a lot of red—red is a negative color for accountants! Also remember that a significant percentage of the population is

color-blind and may not be able to easily find the "green" portion of a chart, so address that with words as well as color.

3. Don't read slides if they are your visual aids. Most people can read and will be annoyed if you simply read to them. Let them read your main points from the slide and augment the key points with your comments.

4. Remember that there are a number of different types of visuals aids that you can use. For example, if a model or a demonstration of the new CRM application or screen shots will work, use it! Variety will help enhance the presentation of what otherwise might be considered boring material.

5. Decide whether handouts will help you during the presentation. You will need to consider the audience and the level of detail people need to walk away with. A general rule is to wait until the end to pass them out so the listeners won't be looking at the handout instead of listening to you. However, that depends on the stakeholder group and your situation.

6. The last point is to practice with the visual aids to make sure they help and not hinder your presentation. For example, if Rod were thinking of demonstrating the screens for the CRM in Project Renewal but the room will not allow everyone to see, it is better to forego the demonstration. Better to make it available for the stakeholder group to view later, perhaps at a terminal somewhere conveniently located near their work area.

The templates in Figure 13.1 may be useful in preparing for your next presentation to a stakeholder group.

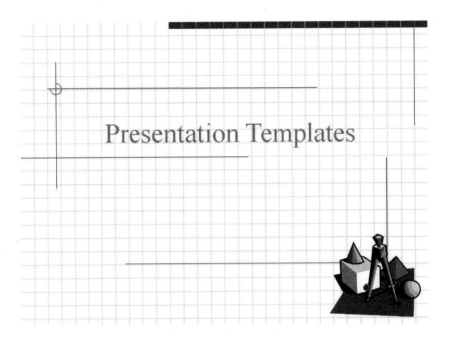

FIGURE 13.1 Presentation templates.

Presentation Planning

AUDIENCE ANALYSIS

KEY INDIVIDUALS	RELATIONSHIP	LEVEL 1-5	CREDIBILITY	QUESTIONS/CONCERNS

Information or Techniques to Gain Acceptance:

Audience Benefits from Presentation:

3

Presentation Planning

SITUATION ANALYSIS

SIZE OF GROUP	
ENVIRONMENTAL FACTORS	
ENVIRONMENTAL CONDITIONS	
INSIDER/OUTSIDER CONSIDERATIONS	

Size of Group: _____   Time of Day: _____

Allocated Time: _____   Location: _____

4

FIGURE 13.1   Presentation templates (*continued*).

Presentation Planning

Audience Checklist- Part 1

- Who plans to attend?

- Who really cares about the project?

- What are their responsibilities?

- Who will be attending that really understands the project?
  Can you preview your presentation with that person?

- Who will be attending that will not understand the project?
  Can you preview your presentation with that person?

- What is his or her relationship to the ideas you are presenting?

- Who created things the way they are today?

5

Presentation Planning

Audience Checklist- Part 2

- Who has won a promotion as a result of the way things are today?

- Who might look bad if things change from the way they are now?

- Why are they attending?

- Who will dislike your ideas? What will they dislike about them?

- Who loses power if things change?

- Who loses access to power if things change?

- Who is most effected by your ideas? How will they be hurt/helped?
  If you assume they will be hurt, how will they be hurt ? If they will be
  helped, how will they be helped?

6

FIGURE 13.1 Presentation templates (*continued*).

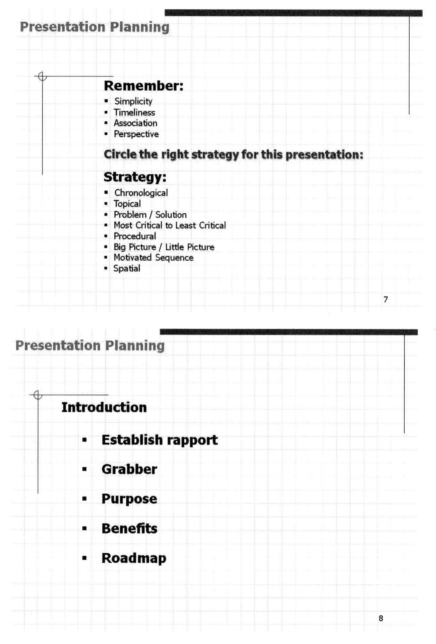

FIGURE 13.1 Presentation templates (*continued*).

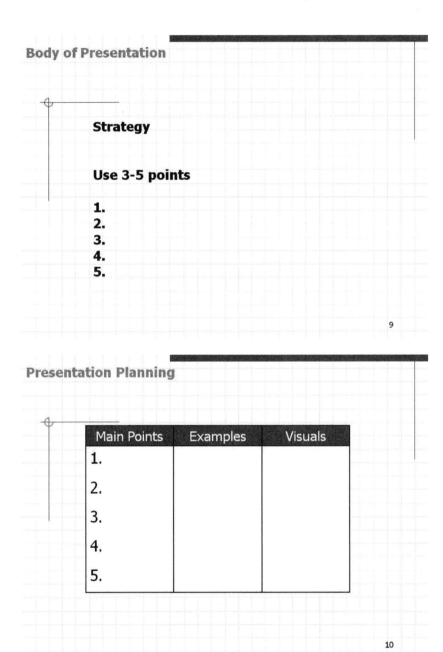

FIGURE 13.1   Presentation templates (*continued*).

Presentation Planning

Questions I need answered

- What new information does IT need?

- Do I need to ask for commitment at the end of the presentation?

- Do I need any information about someone's attitude?

- Do I know enough about the audience's level of commitment?

- Have I done enough to pre-sell my ideas?

11

FIGURE 13.1   Presentation templates (*continued*).

Key Points to Remember

- Make sure you have a clear purpose in mind.
- Review your stakeholder analysis to target the presentation.
- Use a strategy that will appeal to the key stakeholders or decision makers.
- Practice your presentation so there are no surprises.
- Analyze the type of question before you decide how to answer.

After making presentations, probably the next greatest challenge for project managers is how to communicate about problems and issues that have raised their ugly heads during the Execute phase. Let's see how Rod Thompson handled those tricky situations in the next chapter!

Chapter 14

Communicating About Problems

Resolving a project management issue or problem does not really occur until all the affected parties understand and agree to support the resolution. An effective solution almost always means highly effective communications. Not everyone affected will be in the discussions around the problem, but all will have a vested interest in the solution.

To begin with, let's go back to the common elements in Chapter 5: Common Elements of All Communications as a backdrop, but tailored to the situation and needs related to issues. Figure 14.1 shows a flowchart for the issue process. The common elements to look at first would be:

- Stakeholder analysis
- Purpose of the communication
- Strategy
- Power bases
- Formal versus informal
- Barriers to communication
- Tools and technology

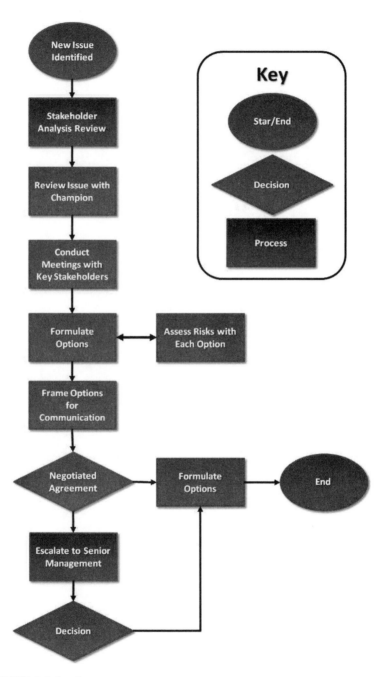

FIGURE 14.1 Issue process.

In determining how to communicate on issues, all of these are important to consider. Issues that arise during a project usually impact a select group rather than the entire stakeholder population (although a universal issue does occur if the product you are trying to deliver just does not work, in which case almost everyone suffers the same fate).

Rod Thompson, our stellar project manager, faced a difficult issue brought to his attention by Joshua Larsen, his technical lead. In briefing Rod, Joshua stated that he believed his technical team and the IT group seemed to be working on some of the same technical tasks for Project Renewal. During the course of a meeting with Luke Johnson, the liaison between Project Renewal and IT, Josh had understood that the IT group was working on the programming of the commissions for sales representatives when the sales reps had offered the customers large discounts. Josh believed his team was responsible for handling the programming for that task. And each group seemed to have been given slightly different instructions on how to address the situation, which complicated the issue even more. There seemed to be a clear breakdown in communications somewhere in the process.

Before deciding how to handle the situation, Rod reviewed his stakeholder analysis and focused on those groups affected by the issue—namely sales, IT, and Human Resources. There were particular sensitivities he needed to consider:

- IT would believe it was responsible for any changes in sales commissions even if Rod's team believed that area was part of its mandate.
- Sales was somewhat fragmented in the way it was organized, so a definite possibility existed that two different people were involved with one person talking with IT and another providing instructions to the Project Renewal team.
- Compensation was clearly within the span of control of HR, so getting that department involved was important to any solution.

Because the issue was both complicated (when you are dealing with people's compensation, it will always be complicated!) and involved several functions, Rod immediately requested a meeting with Paula Dahlberg, his champion. Paula knew many of the key players in sales and Human Resources, but was not as familiar with the IT people. Rod did not request any help from Paula, but had a suspicion that Paula's help would be required later on—either to help resolve the situation or to escalate the issue to Lise Ramsay, the sponsor from the executive team.

Rod then began a series of meetings to uncover the concern and understand the status of the programming from each group's perspective. His plan was to identify the right people and get them in a room together at some point and resolve the problem. However, given the sensitivities he had identified earlier, he knew that requesting a meeting too early would scuttle his chances of resolving the issue and he would be forced, by default, to escalate the issue to Lise Ramsay. His goal was to resolve it and keep Lise out of the situation and above the fray on this subject.

> During the execution phase of a project, the role of the sponsor is more passive than active. The sponsor should provide assistance to the project manager on an "as needed" basis except for routine status briefings.
> *Harold Kerzner, Ph.D.*[1]

Effective Meetings

Rod was painfully aware of the problems with meetings at MedTech. He scrolled through them in his mind:

- No goals or agenda
- Too lengthy
- Poor or inadequate preparation
- Inconclusive

---

[1]Harold Kerzner, *Project Management: A Systems Approach to Planning, Scheduling, and Controlling*, 7th ed. (New York: Wiley, 2001).

- Disorganized
- Started late

He was determined to avoid those traps and run effective meetings so he could resolve the matter as quickly as possible. His team had enough work to do, and he could not afford duplicate work within his project, and he doubted IT could afford it either.

So Rod started with separate meetings with IT, HR, and sales. His agenda was straightforward:

- Goal: Understand the involvement of each group related to the issue of responsibility for programming sales commissions
- Agenda items:
  1. Understand who requested the work for each group.
  2. Status of the effort.
  3. Understand how much effort they
     - had already expended on the work.
     - would require to complete the job as they understood it.
  4. Their perspective on how to best resolve the issue.

He started and ended the meetings on time and had Jessie Cooper, a business analyst on the project working sales issues, in the meetings to record the discussion and capture the key points. He wanted Jessie there in case he needed help in interpreting some of the sales jargon that might come up during the meeting. Before the meetings ended, Rod would ask Jessie to review the key points for clarity and remind anyone who was taking away an action item that he or she had committed to that action by the deadline for completion.

As he suspected, the two teams had been given slightly different instructions because they had come from two different people. The variations were minor in Rod's mind, but it meant that whichever team ultimately became responsible for the programming would have to go back and do some rework once the discrepancies were addressed. Another result from the meetings was a sense that the IT group was actually farther along in the work than the Project Renewal team was. While the IT group claimed it was ahead of his team in the programming, Rod was painfully aware that the IT group was notorious within MedTech for missing schedules and milestones in its projects.

Rod decided to work through the options with Paula Dahlberg. Here is how he framed up the options:

1. Option 1: Project Renewal accepts the responsibility for the programming. This would give Rod the most control over both the schedule and the quality of the work. However, this option would mean the issue would need to be escalated to Lise Ramsay because the IT folks made it clear they would not relinquish the work without a fight.
2. Option 2: Let the IT group accept responsibility for the programming. Rod could accept this option if his technical lead, Joshua Larsen, was given a quality assurance role by the IT team. Rod wanted to ensure the work being done would fit the requirements for Project Renewal. And Josh could also give him advance notice if it appeared IT would not make its milestones.

As he expected by framing the options the way he did, Paula recommended Option 2. He calculated, correctly, that Paula

> To get others to do what you want them to do, you must see things through their eyes.
> *David J. Schwartz*[2]

would not want to escalate the problem to Lise. Another reason Option 2 appealed to Rod was the impact of the rework on his schedule. He was afraid the rework might cause some delays, and he was not anxious to miss a milestone. However, if the IT group missed its timeline, it could also impact the project, so Rod would have to enter this as a risk on his risk register and monitor the situation carefully.

---

[2]David J. Schwartz, *The Magic of Thinking Big* (New York: Prentice-Hall, 1965).

Paula agreed to meet with the IT group, and include Rod, to ne-gotiate the settlement of the issue. She would push the concession by Project Renewal with an insistence on Josh's playing a quality assur-ance role with that team. They would hammer out Josh's role dur-ing the meeting so there would be no misunderstandings later on.

Paula knew that Dan Cohen, the Director of IT, would not be excited by the prospect of having one of Rod's people overseeing the quality of the work within his team, so she met with Dan in ad-vance. She framed the concessions by Rod and Project Renewal (and her concession as the project champion) and essentially made it difficult for Dan to veto the solution. Essentially, Dan was given the message that if he did not accept the compromise, he would face a fight that would go to the executive team. Paula realized that Dan would not want that to happen just as Paula had not wanted it.

Dan relayed the compromise to his project manager and di-rected him to arrange several working sessions with Rod's team to facilitate the handover of the work and manage the reconciliation of the requirements.

By using effective communications on an individual level and a group level (through the meetings he conducted), Rod was able to navigate through a difficult subject and arrive at a solution that everyone could support.

Key Points to Remember

- Review the common elements for communication and apply them to issue communication.
- Identify the stakeholder(s) affected and target the response and the communication.
- Involve your champion as soon as possible and practical, and try to resolve the issue without involving the sponsor if at all possible.
- Communication around problems will usually involve meet-ings, so run them effectively and efficiently.

- Carefully frame the options for solving the predicament so you end up with a solution that you can deliver.

Another difficult situation for a project manager is when the customers or users want to "change horses in the middle of the race"—in other words, change the scope of your project. Just like problems, there is a way to communicate in those situations and still control things.

Chapter 15

Communicating Scope Changes

One of the most difficult challenges for any project manager comes when the scope of the project changes. A few years back, I was asked by a client to help a young man get his project back on track. In assessing the situation, this highly skilled professional had done many aspects of the job very well, but he had not developed a defined process for handling and communicating scope changes. As a result, when a request for a scope modification had been received by his team, he had no way to work with the various stakeholders on what to do or whether to do it at all. As a result, the initiative stalled out, missed key milestones, and threatened the career of this fine young man. I learned some lessons in dealing with that situation, and dozens of others just like it, and those messages are in this chapter. First of all, I would encourage all of you to have a definite process to follow for any similar requests because the process is important as part of communicating to stakeholder groups and managing their expectations.

Basic Assumptions

As project manager, the basic assumption is that you have a scope statement and have tasked your team to do certain work packages based on the requirements and specifications. From whatever sources, there is now a request to change the span or scale of the project.

Rod Thompson, the project manager for Project Renewal, had carefully drafted a process for handling requests for scope changes (Figure 15.1). He had been a part of projects in the early part of his career that had gotten completely

> Scope statement—a common understanding among all stakeholders about the scope and the goals of the project.
> *Project Management Body of Knowledge* (PMBOK)[1]

out of control, and he had a sense that scope control was a key factor. He had seen project managers, in an attempt to please all the stakeholders, who had taken a request and simply built the expanded work into the project. Several things had happened as a result, but usually the project either ran out of money before it finished or had blown through the schedule, or both. It had been a hard lesson, but he had learned it!

The process Rod developed with the Working Committee was simple but effective. A change request could come from a variety of sources, but the first part was within the project team. They would

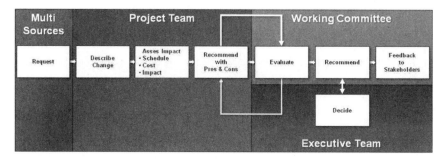

FIGURE 15.1   Process for scope changes.

---

[1]*Project Management Body of Knowledge* (Newtown Square, PA: Project Management Institute, 2003), section 5.2.3.1, p. 110.

develop a clear description of the nature of the change. Then the project team would conduct an impact analysis of the request on the schedule, cost, and quality for Project Renewal. They would also assess how the change might impact the business case by conducting a high-level cost/benefit analysis. Based on the alternatives available for the alteration, the project team would recommend a course of action for the Working Committee with the pros and cons of any and all options. Figure 15.2 illustrates balance of decision parameters.

From there, the Working Committee would evaluate the recommendation along with the analysis the project team provided. Once there was consensus on the recommendation related to the scope change, the Working Committee would send that recommendation to the executive team for a decision. At Rod's urging, Lise had reserved the decisions on scope changes for the executive team since nearly any change involved more cost and a potential to alter the schedule.

After the executive team made a decision, it would pass it back to the Working Committee. The Working Committee would be responsible for communicating the decision to the stakeholders within the functional areas they represented.

Rod had to use the process described in Figure 15.1 when Dan Cohen, Director of IT, approached him about a reworking of the project. Dan learned, from the vendor MedTech has chosen for the

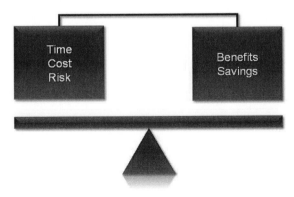

FIGURE 15.2 Integrity of the change.

> ## Key Objectives for Change Control
> 1. To define what the project manager can and cannot do when a change of scope request occurs.
> 2. To establish an agreed-upon process for submitting the change and evaluating its impact on the current project baseline.
> 3. To show how to approve or disapprove—based on sound business principles—the time, effort, and money required for the change.
>
> *Joan Knutson and Ira Bitz*[2]

CRM system, that a new release was coming out in the near future with many of the functions MedTech had originally wanted, but could not get with the current version. Dan believed the Project Renewal team should immediately begin to work with the vendor on the new version and stop work on the existing version.

> Our dilemma is that we hate change and love it at the same time; what we really want is for things to remain the same but get better.
>
> *Sydney J. Harris,*
> *American journalist*

Rod only consented to use the agreed-upon process and investigate Dan's suggestion. However, Rod was equally clear that he would not commit to the new version without an investigation on the impact to the project and, more importantly, without the explicit approval of the leadership team.

Requesting a Change

Rod asked Dan to submit a formal change request to begin the process. Rod also suggested that Dan needed to involve both Luke

---

[2]Joan Knutson and Ira Bitz, *Project Management: How to Plan and Manage Successful Projects* (New York: AMACOM, 1991), p. 97.

PROJECT CHANGE REQUEST

ASSIGNED CHANGE REQUEST NUMBER: _____ [1]

☐ **APPROVED**   ☐ **REJECTED**

Date: _____   [1]See Change Log for next available sequence number.

Change Authorization Decision Required (Date/Time):

Description of Change Requested: (*Attach any additional documentation required to access necessity for change*)

Justification for Change: (*Include the reasons for the change as well as the consequences if the change is rejected*)

Cost Impact:	Schedule Impact:

Other Impacted, Replanning Activity Required: (*Attach supporting documentation*)

Submitted By:	*Printed Name*	*Signature and Date*	
Project Sponsor:	*Approval Signature & Date (if req'd)*	Project Manager:	*Approval Signature and Date*

Johnson, the liaison with the IT group, and Paul Ryan, the lead business analyst, in the discussions so their input could be considered.

The form that Dan would need to complete to start the process for a change in scope is shown on page 181.

Communicating About a Change

Rod's first communication task was to instruct the project team, in conjunction with the IT team, to complete an analysis of the variation in scope. He explained that he needed a thorough estimate from them of any additional work involved. In addition, the work needed to be broken into high-level work packages with any dependencies so he can work those dependencies into a revised schedule. Rod also asked the project team to review the baseline project plan and give him an estimate of the work eliminated by the change so he can factor that into his estimates. Ultimately, Rod was looking to understand the impact on his schedule and his budget if he goes ahead with the new CRM release. So the analysis wouldn't become too large a distraction for the team, Rod gave them a week to complete everything. He would not devote any more time than that.

Rod also asked Paul Ryan to review the business case for the project and see how the change would impact the financial return the executive team expects from Project Renewal. Even though Rod would do his own analysis of the impact on ROI and the business case, comparing his estimates and assumptions with Paul's would give him a reality check before he presented anything to the leadership team. If there were major discrepancies, he would work with Paul to sort them out before he provided anything to the group of executives.

Once the analysis of the work packages for the change was completed, Rod worked to refine and draft a new schedule. Then he analyzed the adjustments in the amount of effort and who on the team would be capable of handling that work so he could assess the impact on his budget. Finally, he asked his quality assurance lead,

Marc Newhouse, to review the amendments for any impacts on the quality of the implementation.

When he had all the information, Rod summarized the transformation to the scope. His work on a revised schedule was complicated by a direction from executive management early on that the project must not interfere with MedTech's year-end closing. The leadership team was afraid of data problems and was not willing to accept that risk. Therefore, Rod's team must finish by the end of the third quarter or extend the schedule to the end of the first quarter of next year.

After completing his analysis, Rod had a meeting and reviewed all the information and his analysis with the project team leads for a sanity check. After asking for certain clarifications, they agreed with his estimates.

Presenting the Options and Reaching a Decision

In completing his assessment, Rod was now ready to present the Working Committee with the information. He would communicate two options for their consideration:

1. Maintain the current plan with no changes since the status quo is the default position for any changes in scope.
2. Rework the project plan, budget the additional money, and implement the new version of the CRM.

For both of these options, Rod would present both the benefits and the risks along with any additional issues the project team had identified. Rod was careful to communicate to the Working Committee that they cannot make this decision, only the executive management can do that. However, he knew the leadership group would be relying on the Working Committee to make a recommendation.

The analysis suggested that Dan Cohen, the IT Director, was correct in suggesting the additional functionality would be desirable for MedTech. However, there would be a schedule slip of six months due to the constraint around year-end. It would also result in additional costs representing an increase of roughly 20 percent to the total cost of the project. So the business decision the Working Committee was faced with, in simple terms, was a balance between the benefits delivered by the newer version versus an increase in the time and cost to complete the project.

Rod also asked the Working Committee to circulate the idea among key people within the functional groups they represent to see if any advantages or disadvantages had been overlooked or underestimated. He also wanted to make sure the business was providing input into the recommendation the Working Committee was making to the management team (as outlined in Chapter 7: Analyzing Changes to Business Process).

One week later, at the Working Committee meeting, the committee debated the merits of the change in scope. To keep the meeting structured and focused, Rod first asked each committee member to report on the discussions with constituents and the general consensus as each member assessed it. Rod wanted to avoid a situation where two or three committee members get into a power struggle, and personalities become entangled with the business decision. By forcing them to articulate their constituents' views, he felt he could keep the debate at the right level. His strategy seemed to work. After debating the situation, the Working Committee decided to recommend that the request for the scope change be rejected. They felt that most of the additional functions would provide additional benefits overall but the need to keep the project on track and within budget outweighed the advantages presented by the newer version.

Rod and Paula Dahlberg, his champion, had alerted Lise Ramsay, the sponsor, that the Working Committee would be debating the scope change request. Lise had asked them to get back with her after the Working Committee had made its recommendation, which they did.

Rod had prepared a small set of slides to give Lise an overview of the request, the process applied to the request, and the ultimate recommendation from the Working Committee. He had the minutes of the Working Committee meeting and all the corresponding backup materials when he and Paula met with Lise. He wanted to be able to answer any questions she had about the basis for the decision. Sure enough, Lise wanted to see the project team analysis and some of the supporting materials the Working Committee had used to make the decision. After reviewing the materials, Lise asked for certain pieces to take with her for the next leadership team staff meeting. She felt confident the leadership team would accept the recommendation of the Working Committee. Before they concluded the meeting, Rod requested that Lise send a formal communication after the leadership team made its decision. He wanted to be able to use that document in the communications to the Working Committee and to the various stakeholders—particularly the IT group, whom he knew would be disappointed in the decision.

Communicating the Decision

When the leadership team confirmed acceptance of the Working Committee recommendation, Rod and Anne Garcia, his communications specialist, drafted a message for the organization. However, before anything went out, Rod made sure he communicated with each member of the Working Committee first. He didn't want anyone to hear about the decision in a secondhand fashion. Also, he met with Dan Cohen, the IT Director, who had first suggested the scope change. He wanted to make sure Dan understood the process that was used and could answer any questions Dan might have about what happened and why. While Dan was disappointed, he commented that the process seemed fair, and it was the first time he felt like he had really been heard in these situations. And he appreciated the process even though the answer was not the one he had hoped for.

Finally, Project Renewal was ready to communicate to the organization about this scope change request. They knew that several groups were aware of the request, and the IT group was particularly keen on learning the decision. Rod and Anne decided to send the message to the organization on the following Monday. Anne drafted a message, and Paula edited it with the help of Anne and Rod for distribution.

Rod had asked Dan Cohen, while they were meeting, if he and Paula could attend his staff meeting on that Monday morning to announce the decision and field any questions. Dan agreed and even coached Rod on some of the questions they were likely to get and some of the attitudes they might see during the course of the meeting. That information allowed Paula and Rod to be prepared to meet with the IT group face-to-face with very rich communications.

Paula and Rod had a similar session with the sales representatives because they were another stakeholder group who would have appreciated some of the new functionality. They asked Gary Stiles, the sales manager on the Working Committee, to join them. Gary might be able to either clarify questions or translate certain elements of the decision in a way the sales reps would accept and/or support.

> The role of a project manager is to manage scope changes, not prevent them!

After they completed all these meetings with specific stakeholders, Rod and Paula sent Anne's communication as a broadcast email message to the organization on behalf of Paula as the champion. The feedback the project team received contained very little resentment and anger, which thrilled them!

Key Points to Remember

- Right from the beginning, have a clearly defined process for scope change—it will make communications much easier.
- Make sure the business is recommending the acceptance or rejection of a scope change, not the project team.

- Your first communication is to your project team on how team members must handle a particular change request.
- An important communication is to the business on the consequences and impact of the change request on the schedule, budget, and/or quality.
- Once the decision is made regarding the scope change, make sure you communicate with both the person or people who requested it and all those who might be impacted by either the acceptance or rejection.

While all this is going on, the users out there are waiting patiently, or impatiently, for something to make their work lives easier. Communicating with them and getting them not only ready, but excited, is a true art form. However, the good news is that you can learn how to do that very successfully!

Chapter 16

Communicating with Operations

Very often in projects, project managers lose sight of the fact that the final product or deliverables will ultimately be transferred to the everyday operations group within the company. In other words, it moves from being a project to being the operating procedure or tool or equipment that people will use every day to help them do their jobs. While there are many tasks that must be completed before handing the project deliverables over to the operations group, one of the most important is the communications that occur to get the operations group ready to receive those deliverables.

In this chapter, I want to cover why it is important to focus on these communications, when the project manager should begin to concentrate on this aspect of communication, and how to communicate depending on the nature of the project. It will also hearken back to Chapter 10: Developing the Communications for the Project.

The first thing to remember in communicating with operations is risk. The greatest fear most operations managers have related to projects is that the project team, and the project manager,

189

will create problems for their Run the Business operations. The concern with business interruptions from a project really centers on the risk to their operating performance measures. It is important to keep in mind that operations managers

> • Never assume that *anyone* knows *anything*.
> • The bigger the group, the more attention must be given to communication.
> • When left in the dark, people tend to dream up wild rumors.
>
> *Hans Finzel*[1]

receive bonuses for hitting their operational targets—missing them puts a portion of their bonus at risk. All projects create risks, and operations managers know that. Many operations managers have also had bad experiences in the past with projects that have hurt them in a variety of ways, so they are not anxious to embrace any project.

When Rod began to execute the communications plan (see Chapter 10: Developing the Communications for the Project), Anne Garcia, his communications expert, gave him some simple guidelines to follow when delivering good news or bad news.

Good News—Bad News

Good News

Anne told Rod that when there is good news to communicate, it is generally delivered early in the message, and usually with a tone of congratulations. He should then explain the consequences of the good news and then follow with any additional details that might make sense for the group he is communicating with. For example, if Project Renewal had conducted some user testing with the CRM system, and the system passed, Rod would start the communication congratulating both the project team members and the users who had volunteered for the testing. They had performed a valuable

---

[1]Hans Finzel, *The Top Ten Mistakes Leaders Make* (Colorado Springs, CO: Cook Communications, 2007), p. 113.

service to MedTech, and their contribution was being recognized in his communication. Rod's communication would also detail the consequences of the passed test as it relates to the readiness of the system to get the other users excited about using the system.

Bad News

Anne's advice was that bad news is generally handled differently. When you are sending bad news, she said, Rod will want to the respect the feelings and previous contributions of those who are receiving the communication and acknowledge them first. Then the writer attempts to frame (remember this from Chapter 12: Using Communications to Handle Risks) the bad news, giving reasons and facts. For example, Rod will have to deliver some bad news to the sales representatives about setting up the CRM. When the systems were reviewed and the current one chosen, one of the features the vendor promised for setting up the CRM system was the ability of sales representatives to upload their contact lists into the system automatically. However, after several tests, the project team was convinced that an automatic transfer cannot occur. They had figured out a workaround using spreadsheets, but it would be much more time consuming for the sales reps. And Rod knew they would not be happy about this development. However, he would give them all the details he had to explain why there was a change and the additional work they would have as a result. He was not trying to "sugar coat" the problem, but he needed the sales reps to keep this situation in perspective. He was worried the sales reps would lose confidence in the system, and his team would lose support from this critical stakeholder group. Therefore, he would also be sure to communicate

> We simply assume that the way we see things is the way they really are or the way they should be. And our attitudes and behaviors grow out of these assumptions.
> *Stephen Covey*

that all the other features promised by the vendor seemed to be working fine. And he would reenforce all the benefits the sales reps would receive when the system was operational.

Dangerous Assumptions

There are three dangerous assumptions that any project manager will need to manage with operations as you communicate with them about your deliverables. They are:

> Assumption 1: Operations does not "own" the preparation for an implementation, the project does.
>
> Assumption 2: Operations will underestimate the complexity and difficulty of getting prepared to accept the project deliverables.
>
> Assumption 3: Operations won't appreciate the time required in creating work process alignment.

Let's look at each of them and how our model project manager, Rod Thompson, handled these during Project Renewal.

Assumption 1: Operations Does Not Own the Preparation for Implementation

Rod ran into this assumption during the course of a Working Committee meeting. Anne Garcia, the communications and change management lead, was outlining the work to prepare the different departments so they would be ready for the CRM system. It became painfully obvious that Gary Stiles did not believe the management team was responsible for preparing the sales team for the implementation of the CRM—in his eyes, it was entirely the responsibility of the project team. Not only did he not see the point, but he felt the management team within sales would not really know how to prepare the sales force.

Rod and Anne realized they had to develop a response to Gary's objections to operations owning the preparation. They developed a strategy centered on the development of what they called "management commitment sessions." This communications effort would involve a series of meetings, starting with the CEO and the executive management team, then cascading its way down through the management ranks to the first-line supervisors. The goal of the sessions would be to help each level of managers develop buy-in with the managers they supervised by communicating a set of specific actions they could use to prepare the managers for the implementation of the CRM at the end of Project Renewal.

Once Rod and Anne completed an agenda and the content of the meetings, they went to Paula Dahlberg, the champion, to get her support. They knew this would be a challenge, since they estimated they would need about two hours to cover the content and get the buy-in they were looking for. Asking managers, from the top down, to set aside two hours would raise objections, and they knew it. The purpose of the meeting was to explain the need for the management commitment sessions, review the proposed agenda, and prepare to take the idea to Lise Ramsay for her endorsement and assistance.

After a review of the workshop and its purpose, Paula agreed to take the idea to Lise. However, Paula wanted the workshop to include a demonstration of the CRM. The discussion about preparation would "wrap around" the demo and be more successful. Because of the potential politics involved in getting Lise involved with another department (sales), Paula asked Rod and Anne to let her handle the discussion alone with Lise. She felt the two of them could be much more candid without the two members of the project team present. Paula did ask Rod and Anne to produce several additional items to help her in describing the problem with Lise, which Rod promised to deliver before the meeting.

Several weeks later, Paula requested a meeting with Rod and told him that Lise had had a meeting with Nick Winters, the Vice President for Sales, and Nick had supported the project's conducting the management commitment sessions. The compromise Lise had to make was reducing the time to 60 minutes. Rod thanked Paula for her help, and he sent Lise an email expressing his appreciation to her as well. He knew it would be difficult for Anne to reduce the time to 60 minutes, but they had few other options. They decided to send out certain information in advance as background materials, hoping that would reduce the amount of time required in the meetings themselves.

During the lessons learned at the end of the project, it was determined that the management commitment sessions had been perceived very positively by the management team—particularly the sales management team!

Assumption 2: Operations Will Underestimate the Complexity and Difficulty of Getting Prepared to Accept the Project Deliverables

A different problem arose within the vendor management and contracts group. Chuck Swindle, who ran vendor management and contracts, was taken aback by the effort required to get his group ready to accept the project deliverables from Project Renewal. When he heard about the amount of time and work Anne Garcia was proposing, his response was "This is a ridiculous amount of time to spend on this. Give the CRM to my people—they are smart, and they will figure it out!"

Rod and Anne developed a slightly different plan for Chuck's group, although they also used the management commitment sessions as a basis for getting buy-in and support. However, the

> The stress that employees often associate with the project deliverables can be traced to
> · Job insecurity
> · Changes in jobs and fear of work overload
> · Lack of communications
> *Vijay K. Verma*[2]

analysis of the business process changes done earlier (see Chapter 7: Analyzing Changes to Business Process) determined there would be a significant impact on the vendor management and contracts people for a few key business processes. Some of the changes to business processes could be built into the communications plan,

---

[2]Vijay K. Verma, *Resource Skills for the Project Manager* (Newtown Square, PA: Project Management Institute, 1996).

and Anne added them to the plan and the schedule. However, others were too complex or significant, and simply communicating those changes would not prepare the vendor management and contracts people for what they were getting into. For those significant changes, Anne and Rod agreed the work in this area would need to be added to the training plan and they completed a Process Documentation Worksheet Figure 16.1). However, they felt the best people to communicate those changes and deliver the training to Chuck's team came from within his group.

With that in mind, Anne worked with Steve Benson, the training specialist, and Chuck to develop a team-teaching program for the vendor management and contracts team. Steve would work with Chuck to pull together the content of the training, and Steve would make sure it was sound from a training perspective. Then Steve and Chuck would work together to assign pairs of people to deliver the training to this group—one training specialist who had the "stand-up" training skills, and another who was considered one of the best in the department to answer those difficult and tricky "what-if" questions that always come up during the training. The training specialist would be responsible for the delivery of

Process	
Activity	
Role	
Staff assignment	

Key Steps	Interactions with Others	Interaction with CRM System or Other Systems
1.		
2.		
3.		
4.		
5.		
6.		
7.		

FIGURE 16.1 Process documentation worksheet.

the standard content, and the vendor management and contracts person would be responsible to answer any technical questions that arose during the training. By being part of the content development, it became much more obvious to Chuck that even with smart people, Project Renewal would require a lot more preparation than simply rolling out the software.

Having the department's "stars" as part of the delivery of training also worked wonders in developing buy-in from the vendor management and contracts people. The training was relevant and specific to their needs, which was critical to its success (more about this in Chapter 17: Preparing Operations to Accept Deliverables).

Assumption 3: Operations Won't Appreciate the Time (and Therefore Money) Required in Creating Work Process Alignment

When Rod first arrived at MedTech a few years ago, one of the things that struck him was the lack of documentation around how work processes were actually peformed at the company. Both to orient himself to the new job of managing projects and to learn more about MedTech as a company, he had asked for documents on standard operating procedures and/or process maps. All he got were policy guidelines, and that was after someone spent the better part of a week trying to locate them! Since that time, Rod has been committed to providing documentation for his projects so he could do his part in filling that void.

He faced a similar challenge with Project Renewal, but it was much larger because of the sheer size of the project. As one aspect of addressing that challenge, he had included the services of a technical writer into his project budget estimate. For most manufacturing facilities, developing Standard Operating Procedures (SOP) was a common practice. However, he knew the person he hired could only go so far in developing an SOP. He or she would need the time and expertise from within the business to complete the documentation.

Therefore, Rod decided he needed to convince the Working Committee to offer help from the business to work with the technical writer on documentation. To be persuasive, he knew from his earlier work with Anne Garcia that he would need to come from a perspective of expertise (see Chapter 10: Developing the Communications for the Project). He decided to ask Walter Fisher for help. Walter is the general manager for manufacturing and oversees the one part of MedTech where process documentation was routinely done and updated. Walter was highly regarded by most people within MedTech (although he could be a little too blunt for some people's taste) and his perspective on why documentation was important and why the business needs to embrace this effort was relevant. Such support would give the effort far more weight than if Rod tried to persuade the Working Committee members.

Rod asked Anne to work with Walter to prepare for his presentation to the Working Committee on the need for documentation so Rod could ask for their support. Anne gathered Rod's thoughts in a separate session so she could include them in the work she did with Walter.

Rod also worked with Paul Ryan, his technical lead, and Luke Johnson, the IT liaison resource, to set up a model office with the CRM application available for people to play with and try out the system. As part of the model office approach, people could log into the project website and provide the project team with feedback and suggestions. While not too many took advantage of the opportunity, the project team did get interesting comments and feedback from those who did.

Symptoms of Misalignment with Operations

The business may exhibit specific symptoms and warning signs that indicate that it is not aligned correctly to receive the deliverables from the project team. Associated communication strategies can help correct the misalignment.

Probably the most common source of misalignment is when the business is not clear on the link between the project and the broader company strategy. Rod became aware of this through one of the feedback loops he established to understand the readiness of the business to receive Project Renewal.

In one of his monthly lunch meetings with key stakeholders (this one happened to be with an accounting manager), he learned the accounting group did not seem to understand the connection between Project Renewal and the broader strategy of MedTech to address the business challenges the company faced. As a result of that meeting, he requested a meeting with Paula Dahlberg and Anne Garcia to develop an in-depth communication strategy to address this problem within the accounting department. Paula was not sure there was a need to be concerned at first, but Rod and Anne discussed consequences of what would happen if accounting did not understand, and therefore support, the efforts of Project Renewal. Rod's biggest concern would be an effort by accounting to change the requirements of the CRM as they worked to move MedTech to the new accounting standards in accordance with the International Financial Reporting Standards (IFRS). Rod was convinced they had considered those requirements, but push-back from accounting could create schedule delays if not handled in a proactive way. At the end of the session, they had a game plan for additional communications for the accounting group. Paula would lead the effort and inform Lise Ramsay of the concern in case they needed to involve her later on.

Build a Storyboard to Explain the Project

The word *storyboard* was coined by filmmakers in the early days of the film industry and commonly referred to a large board holding sketches that depicted step-by-step plot progressions. As with the Hollywood counterpart, a project storyboard can provide a series of images that represent key deliverables and significant facts. Figure 16.2 is an example of the storyboard that Rod and Anne developed for explaining how Project Renewal was going to change the way MedTech operated (the Common Operating Model) to a new way of working.

Operating Model for Medtech (example)

	Sales	Moving and Tracking	Settlements	Contract Administration	Accounting	Managing the Business
Front Office — Sales, Marketing						
Mid Office — Credit, Logistics						
Back Office — Settlements, Contracts				How the Work Gets Done (Activity)		

What the Business Does (Process)
Who Does the Work (Organization)

2009 Effects of Project Renewal on COM (illustrative)

	Sales	Moving and Tracking	Settlements	Contract Administration	Accounting	Managing the Business
Front Office — Sales, Marketing	Check market & credit risk through personal contact; Complex deals personally walked through credit check; Inventory managed in SAP; Real-time view of inventory; Pre-approvals for traders on credit/EOD exposures; Forward profiles					
Mid Office — Credit, Logistics				Exposures on spreadsheets; Limited scalability; Positions entered at end of month; Information available & accurate within hours; Global exposure maximizing opportunity with a common view; Automated exposure calculations; TC becomes analytical, with future curves & "What if tools"		Source data managed locally with local naming conventions
Back Office — Settlements, Contracts	Manual reconciliation of data entry discrepancies for inventory	Manual provisional pricing invoicing; Manual settlements processes using spreadsheet; Accountability for value-added reporting & analysis	3-way reconciliations; Highly transactional; TC with link to SAP including inventory; Highly automated		Positions entered at end of month; Information available & accurate within hours	

2008 Example of a Hotspot for Project Renewal (illustrative)

	Sales	Moving and Tracking	Settlements	Contract Administration	Accounting	Managing the Business
Front Office — Sales, Marketing	Inventory managed in SAP; Real-time view of inventory; Pre-approvals for traders on credit EOD exposures; Forward profiles	Reports of inventory movement delayed by up to 5 days				Source data managed locally with local naming conventions
Mid Office — Credit, Logistics			Hotspot: multiple affects on same people	Limited scalability; Positions entered at end of month; Exposures on spreadsheets; Information available & accurate within hours; Global exposure maximizing opportunity with a common view; Automated exposure calculations; TC becomes analytical, with future curves & "What if tools"		
Back Office — Settlements, Contracts	Manual reconciliation of data entry discrepancies for inventory	Accountability for value-added reporting & analysis; Settlements in SAP highly automated	3-way reconciliations; Highly transactional; TC with link to SAP including inventory; Highly automated		Positions entered at end of month; Information available & accurate within hours	

FIGURE 16.2 Storyboard examples.

In spite of the assumptions that operations might have about who is responsible for getting them ready, good communications will allow a project manager to develop buy-in and involvement. Use a variety of techniques to inform them and prepare them for the deliverables your project is providing!

Key Points to Remember

- Never make assumptions about what people know and don't know.
- The bigger the group, the more attention must be given to communication.
- When left in the dark, people tend to dream up wild rumors.
- Operations managers are very averse to risk, so your communications will need to reflect that sensitivity.
- Deliver good news and bad news differently.
- Operations will make assumptions about how easy, or hard, it is to prepare for your project deliverables, and your communications must manage those assumptions.
- Use a storyboard to explain a long-term project or program.
- Monitor potential misalignment within operations and manage stakeholder expectations with effective communications.

One of the greatest challenges in project management is overcoming the resistance to change that a project will deliver. Communications are a key tool, and you will see the benefits in the next chapter.

Chapter 17

Preparing Operations to Accept the Deliverables

In defining a project, the Project Management Institute reminds us that all projects have a distinct beginning and end. Starting from that description, we are reminded that much of the work completed during a project becomes incorporated into the day-to-day functions of the business. Therefore, as project managers, we must carefully plan and prepare for the day when the project ends and operations take over. That will be the focus of this chapter.

First of all, let's review three key requirements for preparing operations that we learned from earlier chapters. They are

1. Communicating how operations will look after the project is completed using a well-developed Case for Change (see Chapter 6: Writing the Case for Change).
2. Analyzing and communicating the changes in work process that will occur (see Chapter 7: Analyzing Changes to Business Process).
3. Understanding the principles of the adoption of project deliverables best illustrated by Napoleon's thirds (the idea that

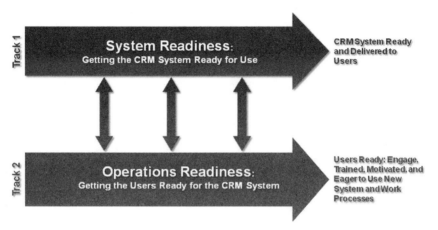

FIGURE 17.1 Dual perspective on operations readiness.

approximately one-third of the people will quickly accept the project, one-third will immediately reject the project, and the remaining one-third will take a "prove-it-to-me" attitude) (from Chapter 9: Developing an Operations Integration Plan).

In addition to these absolute requirements, there are two more:

1. Providing operations with any training that will be needed to be successful.
2. Communicating how personnel will be evaluated on performance after implementation.

In actual fact, you could almost think of them as two separate projects that run on parallel tracks until the end (Figure 17.1).

Providing the Training Operations Needs to Be Ready

Very often project managers take a superficial look at training and ask the question, "What will people need to *know* to make the project work?" I would suggest that executing the training plan should focus on this question instead, "What will people *need to be able to do* to make the project successful?" Focusing on *doing* rather than *knowing* is a critical difference. It changes the paradigm from a learning solution to a job-related solution. Basically, people *do* work, hence the focus on doing rather than knowing (see Chapter 7: Analyzing Changes to Business Process). Follow the plan for functional training and competency training during the project execution.

Rod Thompson used another successful tactic for delivering the training. He worked with Steve Benson and his champion, Paula Dahlberg, to identify people within the key stakeholders to act as co-trainers with Steve. Where possible, they wanted to use people who had the platform skills to actually conduct the instruction with Steve's support. For these employees, Steve conducted a series of workshops to train the trainers and give them additional skills to deliver the workshop—they already had the technical job skills. These train-the-trainer sessions also gave this group of subject matter experts the experience with CRM to answer most of the questions that might come up during the lessons. All of the people identified were vetted with the appropriate Working Committee members so they would support these experts too.

Where the group could not identify a person with the potential platform skills within a particular group, it devised another approach. Steve would assume the lead instructor role for delivering the training. To support Steve, the group identified a subject matter expert within the key stakeholder group who would attend the class to answer those "tricky" technical questions that might be beyond Steve's ability to answer. Steve conducted a separate workshop for this group of SMEs to explain how the training would be conducted, review the content of the materials, and hand out the script for how they would support him during the training.

In line with the use of modules as outlined in Chapter 7: Analyzing Changes to Business Process, the Working Committee worked with Steve Benson and Paula Dahlberg to identify which modules each of the job title groups within their area of responsibility should complete to prepare for the CRM at the end of the project. They developed a matrix that allowed supervisors to quickly identify which modules would be required for each of their people. The matrix also convinced various operations groups that the training would not be a waste of time and would be targeted directly to their work.

The final step was to address the issue of certification with the Working Committee. Rod's experience in the past was that day-to-day activities always seemed to get in the way of the courses. People would use excuses to either miss the training or try to avoid it altogether. He was determined to make sure everyone was ready.

Rod wanted to make the training mandatory and make sure no one would be allowed to log on to the CRM system without being properly prepared. He discussed the idea with Lise Ramsay and Paula Dahlberg in advance to make sure he had their support. He wanted to not only have training that counted attendance, but that ensured that people could properly use the system. He wanted Steve Benson to develop a simple but effective test for this purpose. The question arose "What if someone fails, what then?" To address that concern, Steve Benson developed a process of allowing individuals to take the test a second time in case there was a simple mistake that caused the problem. However, if someone failed again, Steve would arrange one-on-one coaching by the subject matter expert for that individual. After the coaching, the person could take the test again. If he or she failed again, the issue would be turned over the manager of that area for resolution.

With that process in place, the Working Committee approved the certification and actually became enthusiastic about the idea. After all, mandatory requirements had become somewhat standard in other situations within MedTech, particularly related to intellectual property and security issues. People would also know how to find the help needed when they either forget or the CRM project deliverables do not behave as they expected after the training was completed.

Anne Garcia then developed a comprehensive communication for the organization regarding the training plan. It explained how the workshops would incorporate information from the process changes as well as technical portions in the

> In business and in football, it takes a lot of unspectacular preparation to produce spectacular results.
> *Roger Staubach, Football Hall of Fame and successful real estate businessman*[1]

use of a software application. She worked with Steve Benson to develop a detailed schedule as well as the modules that each key stakeholder group would be expected to attend. Before the communication was released to the broader organization, the Working Committee reviewed and approved it. This served as a way to make sure nothing was overlooked and as a way to keep the Working Committee informed in case its help was needed later to get reluctant people to the seminars.

Rod also decided to use another idea to prepare operations and keep people connected to the project deliverables. The idea was to identify people at various locations within each stakeholder group to support the project. These people would be recruited by the Working Committee members and identified as a Single Point of Accountability (nicknamed by a wag in the Working Committee as "Spocks" after the *Star Trek* character because of the abbreviation SPOC).

These people would serve as the vehicle for preparation with various stakeholder groups. The SPOCs would be people within

> The SPOCs are additional business people beyond the Working Committee members. In the case of MedTech, they represent groups such as sales, marketing, and so on in each of MedTech locations globally.

---

[1]Glenn Van Ekeren, *Speaker's Sourcebook II* (Upper Saddle River, NJ: Prentice Hall, 1994), p. 301.

various parts of the business who would use a checklist Rod and his team developed to monitor if everyone in each location was ready. The checklist included such items as:

- Has everyone attended training?
- Are all of them certified?
- Does this location have the backup materials developed for answering go-live questions?

If there were any missing entries, the SPOC would contact his or her Working Committee member and alert him or her to the situation (for example, not everyone was trained or certified). Finally, Rod had to work with Luke Johnson, his liaison with IT, and Dan Cohen, the Director of Information Technology, to ensure the proper support was in place for the project deliverables after the CRM moved into general operations. In Rod's experience, too many projects could not properly close out because the ongoing support was not prepared to accept its responsibility at the conclusion of the project. It led to scope creep and eroded both the project budget and schedule if not handled correctly. And inevitably the project reputation suffered, even though it was not the project's responsibility to provide operations support.

Performance Evaluation and Project Deliverables

One of the biggest obstacles Rod faced in preparing operations for the deliverables from Project Renewal centered on getting management to agree to hold users of the CRM system accountable. Rod believed in the basic principle of accountability—if you want people to use the system properly, their managers must *expect* that from them. However, Rod realized that getting management to agree to the accountability was easier said than done.

His first step was to work with Paula Dahlberg as champion on a strategy for gaining approval from the executive team. Both of them realized they would need Lise Ramsay's help, but they would need to come to her with a plan.

The first element in the plan centered on the training certification. If they could get the agreement of the senior management to demand a passing score on the simple user test after training, it would be a small step to a broader accountability. Since the Working Committee had recommended the certification and the process for remediation if required, Rod and Paula felt confident they could get senior management to the next level.

They also realized they were treading into the responsibility of Human Resources. They would need to engage George Maxwell, the Vice President for Human Resources at MedTech. Without George's buy-in, the executive team would never approve any changes to the performance appraisal system used at MedTech. Rod and Paula were certain that Lise's first question would be George's position on the issue. As a result, Paula requested a meeting with George to discuss Project Renewal and the implications to HR.

As expected, George agreed to the meeting but was initially unclear why he would be involved in a discussion related to project deliverables from the CRM system. Rod and Paula anticipated this question, so they prepared a small presentation (based on the principles of identifying the purpose, preparing according to a strategy most likely to be successful with George, and anticipating his objections as outlined in Chapter 13: Presenting to Stakeholders During the Project Execution) to provide George the background on the issue and the support they were hoping for. They came out of the meeting with an action to work with one of George's directors, Annette Springer, on the details of what implementation

> One of the hardest lessons . . . to internalize is the primacy of departmental loyalties and self-interest over organization-wide concerns.
>
> *Jeffery K. Pinto*[2]

---

[2]Jeffery K. Pinto, *Power, Politics, and Project Management* (Newtown Square, PA: Project Management Institute, 1998), p. 262.

would require. They all agreed to come back in three weeks to discuss the results of the work and the feasibility of changing the performance evaluation system.

Rod and Paula knew they would have to tread carefully with Annette because Annette was the person primarily responsible for the current performance evaluation system. She would not take kindly to any hints the current system was not working (a sensitivity as discussed in Chapter 5: Common Elements for All Communications). Their approach was to frame the changes as a refinement of the current system, which they viewed as working well for MedTech. The approach worked, and Annette helped them work through the details of implementation. Rod also briefed the Working Committee on the work being done with HR so members would feel informed—and he invited them to provide any input to the revised process as it was designed.

When the follow-up meeting with George Maxwell occurred, Annette was there supporting the new performance evaluation approach related to Project Renewal. As they expected, after asking some questions and challenging several points, George agreed to support the changes and would do so with the senior management team.

Rod and Paula were now ready to go to Lise Ramsay. Again, using the principles outlined in Chapter 13: Presenting to Stakeholders During the Project Execution, Rod and Paula prepared a brief presentation for Lise, giving her the background on the issue, the agreement achieved with HR, and the action they required from her—namely, bringing the issue before the executive team for its agreement to support an expanded performance evaluation based on the project deliverables from Project Renewal. After requesting a few additional items as backup and scheduling a meeting with George Maxwell to discuss the recommendation, Lise was ready to put the item on the agenda of the leadership team meeting. Paula also recommended to Lise that she socialize the idea with some of the key leaders such as Nick Winters, VP of Sales, in advance of the meeting.

To no one's surprise, Nick had already become aware of the recommendation by Gary Stiles, the sales manager on the Working Committee. Therefore, he was not surprised when Lise requested a discussion. More important, he was quite willing to support the idea with several minor changes based on input from his sales managers.

When the issue finally made it to the agenda of a leadership team meeting, the outcome was a foregone conclusion. There were some questions, but overall, the executive team lined up in support of the new performance evaluation scheme.

The final step in the process was to determine how to best communicate the decision to the company personnel. Rod and Paula worked to Anne Garcia, the communications specialist, on a variety of options. They considered

1. Sending an announcement.
2. Including it in the training.
3. Making it an element of the management commitment sessions (see Chapter 16: Communicating with Operations).

After considering the pros and cons of each, they decided it really would make the most sense to pull it into the management commitment sessions. After all, these were the communications meetings where people at all levels were discussing Project Renewal with their immediate supervisors. All agreed it was the appropriate venue for this type of decision.

Anne was then given the action to go back and rework the agenda for the management commitment sessions to include the decision and details related to the change in performance evaluation for MedTech employees using the CRM system.

Readiness Assessment Checklist (Figure 17.2)

Readiness Checklist
for Project Renewal

Instructions

The Readiness Checklist uses a standard set of 20 questions that cover the essential sources of readiness that may create project risk. We want to use your answers, and the answers of others in your asset team, to these questions as a way to assess any risks to the success of Project Renewal as we move to roll-out the Customer Relationship Management (CRM) system. It is the responsibility of the Champion and the Project Manager to evaluate the results of the Readiness Checklist in order address and manage any project related risks. We will provide a summary of the responses to the Single Point of Contact (SPOC) within your group.

In this tool a 7-point scale is used for each answer. In this 7-point answer scale, 1 is the most negative response, indicating a high level of concern over the readiness of people to accept the CRM tool; 4 is a neutral response, indicating that your team does not know or has not yet formed an attitude or opinion about that question; and 7 is the most positive response, indicating an attitude that suggests strong readiness and support for a successful implementation.

Completing the Assessment

To answer each category question use your mouse to highlight and underline a number on each answer scale. *For example:*

1. **Case for Change/Direction** To what extent is the Project Renewal Case for Change understood?	Not At All 1 2	No View 3 4 5	Very Much 6 7

Readiness Checklist

Component – Category Question	Answer Scale
Leadership	
1. **Case for Change/Direction** How well does the team understand the reasons for implementing the CRM?	Not At All / No View / Very Much 1 2 3 4 5 6 7
2. **Motivation** How motivated do I believe my manager is to complete this CRM system implementation successfully?	Not At All / No View / Very Much 1 2 3 4 5 6 7
3. **Leadership** To what extent has there been visible management leadership for Project Renewal?	Not At All / No View / Very Much 1 2 3 4 5 6 7
4. **Commitment** How important do I think Project Renewal is to my management?	Not At All / No View / Very Much 1 2 3 4 5 6 7
Organizational	
5. **Ability and Resources** To what extent is this team ready to commit the effort needed to use the CRM effectively?	Not At All / No View / Very Much 1 2 3 4 5 6 7
6. **Rewards** To what extent will people be rewarded for using the CRM?	Not At All / No View / Very Much 1 2 3 4 5 6 7
7. **Performance Evaluation** To what extent is this team willing to change the way people are evaluated on their job performance to accommodate the use of the CRM in the future?	Not At All / No View / Very Much 1 2 3 4 5 6 7
8. **Team Work** Will the CRM enable improved collaboration between groups within MedTech?	Not At All / No View / Very Much 1 2 3 4 5 6 7
9. **Process Change** Will the CRM combined with a revised business process help you be more efficient in your work?	Not At All / No View / Very Much 1 2 3 4 5 6 7
10. **Competition** To what extent will using the CRM give us an advantage in managing our business that our competitors do not have?	Not At All / No View / Very Much 1 2 3 4 5 6 7
11. **Culture** To what extent is using the CRM consistent with our team's culture?	Not At All / No View / Very Much 1 2 3 4 5 6 7
12. **Compatibility** To what extent is Project Renewal consistent with helping MedTech achieve our business targets?	Not At All / No View / Very Much 1 2 3 4 5 6 7
Team	
13. **Roles/Responsibilities** To what extent is your team confident about the changes in their responsibilities after the completion of Project Renewal?	Not At All / No View / Very Much 1 2 3 4 5 6 7
14. **Career Opportunities** To what extent will the project increase career opportunities for you and your co-workers?	Not At All / No View / Very Much 1 2 3 4 5 6 7
15. **Technical Support** To what extent is your team confident that they have the technical support needed to succeed after the CRM is implemented?	Not At All / No View / Very Much 1 2 3 4 5 6 7
16. **Training** How confident is your team in the training that you have received for using the CRM effectively?	Not At All / No View / Very Much 1 2 3 4 5 6 7
17. **Workload** To what extent is your team confident that the the CRM will help them do their work more effectively?	Not At All / No View / Very Much 1 2 3 4 5 6 7

Comments

Please write any comments you have regarding the ISIS implementation that we have not asked about and any comments you have about this readiness checklist and/or your responses to the questions.

FIGURE 17.2

Communicating with Managers

Managers have different orientations (the way they look at the world), creating different needs for communicating with them. There are positive and negative aspects to each orientation and that orientation, which can often be situational. However, here are some tips on what each style of manager needs from you as the project manager.

People-Oriented Managers

Positive characteristics include their genuine concern for others; they are usually nonjudgmental. For the people they work for, they generally provide clear verbal and nonverbal feedback and will notice others' moods quickly. They are also interested in building relationships, including with people on the project.

However, there can be a negative side to these same managers. For example, they may get overly involved with others' feelings and internalize their emotional states. That can be a problem if your project creates stress or anxiety within their people. Also, they are prone to avoiding seeing the faults in others. They may become overly expressive when giving feedback and may not be discriminating enough in building relationships.

Given these characteristics, what do they need from you? First of all, give them facts and use logic when you communicate with them. When you speak to them personally, you must be direct and concentrate on the tasks or commitments you need from them. You must respect their sincerity and, above all, demonstrate individual follow-through when you make promises to them.

Action-Oriented Managers

Another distinct group are those who are action-oriented. Their positive characteristics include the ability to get to the point quickly and give clear feedback. They will be very good at concentrating on understanding the task at hand and can help people who might be seconded to your project focus on what is important. They will encourage others to be organized and will identify inconsistencies in communications you have with them, so beware!

On the negative side, this group of managers will tend to be impatient. They may have a tendency to jump ahead and finish the thoughts of others. They can get distracted by unorganized speakers or disorganized communications. In situations such as the management commitment session, they may be prone to ask blunt questions and may appear overly critical. Also, they may minimize relationships and the personal concerns of their staff.

Given these characteristics, what do they need from you? They will need you to be flexible in your work procedures and be clear about the priorities for them and their team. You will also need to appear very organized, or they will dismiss you out-of-hand and create a poor environment for your project deliverables.

Content-Oriented Managers

This group of managers will value technical information. They will constantly test your communications for clarity and understanding. They have a tendency to encourage others to provide support for their ideas, so they will expect the same from you. Overall, they will welcome complex and challenging information and can analyze all sides of the issue.

On the negative side, this group of managers may be overly detail-oriented and, in fact, get bogged down in detail and miss the big picture. Be aware that these people may intimidate others by asking pointed questions, so be prepared when you communicate with them. Also, they may very well minimize the value of non-technical information and/or discount information from non-experts, so keep that in mind when you communicate with them. Finally, this group can take a long time to make decisions because they do have a tendency to go to the details and feel the need to analyze everything from all the angles.

Given these characteristics, what do they need from you? You will need to let them know if any actions on their part are time sensitive or if they need to make quick decisions. If you can, try to compromise with their opposition on some of the details of the project.

Be sensitive in communications with them by using recognized experts (these can be respected internal people) to deliver messages to them.

Time-Oriented Managers

This group of managers is very conscious about managing their time and others. You may need to set time guidelines for meetings and conversations by letting them know in advance about any time requirements they may have. When people are speaking to this group of people, they will discourage "wordy" speakers and will often give cues to others when time is being wasted.

The negative side for this group is the tendency to be impatient with time. They are prone to interrupt when others are speaking or not really "read" written communications sent to them. They can also let time affect their ability to concentrate on tasks and rush others working with them by frequently looking at watches or clocks. This can create an artificial limit on the creativity of others by imposing time pressures.

Given these characteristics, what do they need from you? To communicate with this group you will need to analyze the risks because of their "rush" to complete work. I would advise you to use caution in dealing with this group and be deliberate before deciding how to communicate with them. And be sure to research your facts before you communicate with this group!

Metaphors

In communicating to managers, you should also pay attention to the metaphors different managers use. You will notice that most people will draw verbal pictures of the world around them and their place in that view of the world. These vivid figures of speech are drawn most commonly from the sports world, literature, television, religion, or other areas of common interest. These images will give you clues as to what these people value and fear, as well as their "rules" of behavior. These metaphors will also reveal an optimistic, pessimistic, or confused outlook on the situation. With that in mind,

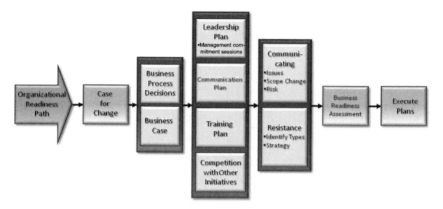

FIGURE 17.3   Preparing operations deliverables.

as you communicate with managers, be aware of the metaphors used by this group, whether individually or collectively.

Preparing operations for the project deliverables is both difficult and time consuming (Figure 17.3). However, the effort and time invested in preparing operations properly will be critical to how the project is ultimately judged.

Key Points to Remember

Training will need to include how people will actually complete their work once the project is turned over to operations.

- Get the business to make a decision on whether certification is appropriate for preparation within operations.
- Provide a complete communication package on the training using SPOCs to deliver the communication.
- Include how people will be evaluated on the job after the project deliverables are moved into operations.
- Remember the importance of middle management and recognize the best way to communicate with them effectively.

Now we'll look at how to overcome the resistance to change as part of planning for any project.

Chapter 18

Overcoming Resistance to Change

This chapter will look at the usual causes for resistance to change and how to deal with those issues effectively. Also, I will detail the types of people who may be encountered during the execution of a project and how to respond to their behaviors, either personally or through the leadership of the organization.

> The individuals who will succeed and flourish will also be masters of change: adept at reorienting their own and others' activities in untried directions to bring about higher levels of achievement. They will be able to acquire and use power to produce innovation.
>
> *Rosabeth Moss Kanter,*
> *author and Harvard*
> *Business School professor[1]*

This chapter will also help the project manager to distinguish between those people who are relatively harmless (e.g., a group I will identify as the "fence sitters") and those who are really dangerous to the success of the project

---

[1]Glenn Van Ekeren, *Speaker's Sourcebook II* (Upper Saddle River, NJ: Prentice Hall, 1994), p. 58.

(e.g., a group I will call the "saboteurs"). I will show how the communication plan combined with a leadership plan and a comprehensive training plan all contribute elements to helping the project manager overcome resistance to change. I will also refer back to preparing the management team introduced in Chapter 2: Preparing the Leadership.

> Organizations have complex, well-developed immune systems, aimed at preserving the status quo.
>
> *Peter Senge et al.*[2]

Here's what we will cover in this chapter along with strategies to address them:

- Reasons for resistance
- Types of resistors
- Overcoming resistance

Reasons for Resistance

Fear

People who operate out of fear of projects and the products and services they deliver are usually seeing only the worst case scenario. During the course of Project Renewal, the Working Committee reported that they were hearing statements like "They aren't going to need all of us after the change, and we're the ones who will be out of a job." "I used to be considered an expert in this area. Now I won't understand the new environment any better than anyone else."

Rod understood this perception often arose from a deeply held belief that people feared they wouldn't be personally competitive after a project was delivered. He answered those concerns with a strong message delivered by the Working Committee members to reassure the business people that the project team would make sure they were well prepared for the CRM system. As well, the message

---

[2]Peter Senge et al., *The Dance of Change* (New York: Currency/Doubleday, 1999).

included a detailed description about the training being offered that provided specific guidance for using CRM in their job roles within MedTech. He made sure there were job aids developed—whether it was a help desk phone line dedicated to CRM questions or actual "cheat sheets" distributed right to people's desks with common instructions and information—that MedTech's people could use when they had questions. Another concern surfaced by the Working Committee—a belief that mistakes would be punished when the new system was rolled out. It came out like this: "MedTech spent a lot of money on this change. The first person to mess up is the first one out the door." To address this fear, Rod worked with Paula Dahlberg and Anne Garcia to build the correct message and incorporate those key points into the management commitment sessions (see Chapter 16: Communicating with Operations). Rod wanted to overcome this particular fear by having everyone hear, directly from his or her boss, that there would be no retaliation for mistakes.

Feelings of Powerlessness

At times when projects create significant changes within the company, such as what Project Renewal was doing for MedTech, there can be a feeling that people's ideas are not valued. The Working Committee reported hearing statements like: "The last time we went through a project like this, I told them how to make it work, and they didn't listen." Or "Management cares only about themselves; the rest of us are in here as laboratory rats. We're not being included in any of this."

To counter this fear, Rod spent part of a Working Committee session explaining to the members that a key function of their role was to address just this type of fear. He explained it was one of the fundamental reasons he wanted to make sure they were seeking input from their groups before making various decisions. He also wanted them to actively advertise the fact that they were soliciting input from key people (not necessarily everyone) so that this type of perception did not occur again. The Working Committee began to see the wisdom of the way Rod was asking them to handle the business decisions affecting their people.

Absence of Self-Interest

Often, overcoming resistance can result in people not perceiving the benefits of the project. This can be particularly true when the benefits are much more long term in nature or primarily benefit others. Rod knew this was a common problem, and he knew how he wanted to address it through communications.

He worked with Anne Garcia to take the Case for Change (see Chapter 6: Writing the Case for Change) and modify it to make it more meaningful for each level of management within MedTech. His goal was to complete the adaptations prior to each management commitment session (see Chapter 16: Communicating with Operations) so it would be targeted for the group attending that workshop. Within each seminar, the managers would review the document in a way that people could really see how the changes would impact them. He made sure to direct Anne not to change the overall direction of the text, but supply a little more granularity as the management commitment sessions progressed through MedTech. It was a way to address not only the standard questions within the Case for Change, but also specifically these questions:

- "What's in it for me?"
- "What are the benefits in the future?"
- "Is this fair or just one more change inflicted on the workers who are doing all the work?"

Types of Resistors

Various types of resistors will pose challenges to the project manager and the project team. They tend to fall along a continuum from those who are not too dangerous to those who are very dangerous.

Our model project manager, Rod Thompson, worked with Anne Garcia, his change management and communications specialist, to identify various key stakeholders and put them into the various camps. They also knew about the continuum, so they decided to rank them accordingly from harmless to those who would destroy the project if they could.

1. The first group they identified was those people who just try to ignore the project and hope it goes away. They typically will quietly oppose the outcome of the project, but not in any overt way. The way Rod and Anne spotted them was based on observations that their actions usually don't match their words when they are asked to do something related to the project. For example, one of the key players in marketing would say, in public, that the CRM was important and everyone needed to support it. However, each time she was invited to attend a meeting related to the system, she would accept the meeting invitation, but not show up at the scheduled time. Rod did not consider this group too dangerous, but he recognized that anyone who was insincere about opposition to the project was a potential problem. Where they were key stakeholders, Rod made sure they received regular visits from the appropriate member of the Working Committee or Paula Dahlberg, the champion. He wanted to make sure they had regular, personal communications so he could confirm they would not turn into resistors that could be more troublesome.

2. Another group on the continuum Rod and Anne identified were those people who won't make up their mind. Rod knew these people were usually very cautious and wanted to be on winning side. They were very political in their orientation. They were usually not too dangerous, but he made sure the members of his project team were aware of these people because they were always looking for the project team to make a mistake, which might give them an excuse to pull back on their support. He knew that he would have to be cautious with this group and make sure he never became overly confident in any of his communications with them.

The exception within this category were those middle-level managers who could have become blockers for the project. Just like the earlier group, he assigned a member of the Working Committee to each of those managers to provide them with frequent, personal communications to win them over.

3. The next group Rod and Anne identified they labeled Dissenters. This group was quite open in their opposition to either the direction of the project or some of the business decisions made by the Working Committee. Rod knew they were strong in their beliefs and in their reasons for opposing certain aspects of Project Renewal. This group would be much harder to control, let alone win over. However, Rod was also careful to recognize these people were knowledgeable, and they might actually identify either a risk or a shortcoming within the details of the project that the project team or Working Committee had missed. Therefore, he was careful to make sure these people were not ignored, but that their comments were carefully evaluated and not just dismissed out of hand. The communications with this small group of people might need to contain a message that contained both a "carrot and stick." To that end, the Vice President of Sales sent out a note that was a classic example of how to achieve that effect. It read:

> The MedTech leadership team is behind this new CRM system 100%. We want to emphasize to everyone our personal support and the importance we give to the project. Going forward, you will be meeting with your direct supervisor to get prepared for supporting and using the new system.

Also Rod assigned some of these people to Paula Dahlberg, his project champion. While that would not change their basic dissent, he knew that Paula had the respect of a broad audience within the company. She also had the political connections with the senior management to make things uncomfortable if these individual managers started to impede the progress of the project. And these dissenters knew that too! While Paula was not excited with the assignment to communicate one-on-one with these people, she did understand why she needed to be the point person and agreed.

4. The last group Rod and Anne identified were the most dangerous. This group was identified as Saboteurs. Rod recognized this group was usually silent to senior management and would not be recognized as such. His experience with these people was they could be especially aggressive and would stab you in the back if they got half a chance. He realized this small number of people, they identified two, must be controlled at all costs. If they were left unchecked, they would spread dissension and discord through rumors and misinformation. He reviewed his assessment with Paula, his champion, to see if they agreed. When Paula concurred with the evaluation Rod and Anne had made, they developed a plan to rein in these individuals.

The plan would be to alert Lise Ramsay of the concern with the idea of an intervention later if required. Paula also identified the immediate supervisors for these two individuals, and she agreed to provide those people with personalized one-on-one communications. The strategy was to keep the record straight with those supervisors as well as keep tabs on the types of gossip the Saboteurs might be formulating to damage the success of the project.

> When people help design new processes, they will be much more likely to use them. The more people contribute to answering the "how" questions, the more they will buy into making the "how" work.
>
> *Steve Robbins*[3]

Overcoming Resistance

- *Ensure all senior managers are on board.* Use your champion and sponsor to make sure the senior team is on board with your project in word *and* deed.
- *Communicate very clearly and make sure all communications are directed a specific people—don't fall into the trap of broadcast emails.* Make sure you describe the nature of expected

---

[3]Steve Robbins, *Communication as a Change Tool: Written Communications That Inform and Influence* (Cambridge, MA: Harvard Business School Press, 2006), p. 93.

changes brought on by the project and provide a clear rationale for those changes. When necessary, use the Case for Change to explain the business case and the potential risks if the project fails.

- *Ensure all mid-level managers/supervisors are on board with the initiative.* Don't forget that these people are the ones who supervise most of the work completed within the business. You will need their support. If they are part of the resistance, develop a strategy for overcoming that resistance.
- *Ensure employees are engaged.* Use your Working Committee as a way to give employees the opportunity to provide

This checklist was developed to help guide you through the implementation of Project Renewal.

Champion Questions	Readiness Assessment	Follow-up Actions
1. Can I explain the benefits of the project and what is at stake for the company?	Yes No	
2. Do I know the project timeline and when each group will be impacted? Have I communicated that to operations?	Yes No	
3. Do I know the changes that will occur as the result of the CRM and how each team and functions will have to do work differently? Have I shared those changes with operations?	Yes No	
4. Have I referred people to the right website location where they can find the latest information?	Yes No	
5. Am I routinely communicating with operations people to share project updates? Am I routinely seeking feedback from operations as the project progresses?	Yes No	
6. Am I proactive and anticipating where there might be bottlenecks or other problems during implementation? Have I suggested alternatives to my Working Committee to address those concerns?	Yes No	
7. Am I talking with various operations groups to understand what they are hearing about Project Renewal?	Yes No	
8. Have I identified and had conversations with people who are negative about the project and asked to understand why they are not supporting the project?	Yes No	
9. Do I know how to get answers from the project team when operations raises issues or questions that I can't answer?	Yes No	
10. Have I identified peak workload times and communicated those to the Training Coordinator? Have I offered scheduling alternatives to ensure that all of my colleagues receive the required training without compromising the performance of the company?	Yes No	

FIGURE 18.1 Champion implementation checklist.

input and then provide feedback on decisions being made as part of the project.

- *Ensure key influencers are on board.* Key influencers do not always have a grand title, but they can help you in selling the deliverables from the project. To engage them, first you will have to find out who they are (see Figure 18.1). Then meet with them informally to seek out their views and engage them without emotion (or use appropriate members of your project team in this role). Afterwards, communicate with them regularly and use them as feedback vehicles for broader communications to the company.
- *Not all resistance to change comes from the same motivation* (for example, fear or helplessness), *nor is it always bad* (don't forget our dissenters who are technically very good).
- *People are much more likely to accept changes from projects if they have been part of designing those changes.*

In conclusion, there are a variety of ways to make people more comfortable by keeping them informed and engaged. The old story about treating people like mushrooms (in the dark) until the last minute just does not work.

Key Points to Remember

- There are a variety of reasons for people to resist changes your project will initiate.
- Resistors tend to fall into four distinct groups; some are more dangerous to your project's success than others.
- Use communications to overcome resistance to the changes brought about by your project.

Another source of problems, including opposition, occurs when various initiatives collide into the company at the same time—often impacting the same people. The next chapter will look at how to handle that situation and the role of communications.

Chapter 19

Handling Competition with Other Initiatives

Every project manager has probably faced the situation where his or her project was suddenly, and unexpectedly, impacted by other initiatives that are going on in the company at the same time. The frustration can mount when your project people are pulled away, causing a slippage in your schedule, and increase when that same program also diverts attention from your very important work. These circumstances may impact the

- Availability of project team members.
- Political climate where all projects live.
- Accessibility to other people as the business prepares for the project deliverables.

The sense of being orphaned without management support or even interest can cause severe morale problems. Communications are a critical success factor in managing the competition from other initiatives.

That's the bad news—the good news is that using appropriate communications can alleviate that situation to keep your work front and center with management. And you can minimize the negative influence on your efforts.

In this chapter we will look how to overcome the problem and then examine specifically how Rod Thompson handled this classic situation during Project Renewal.

There are some key principles that all project managers must adhere to if they are to be successful in managing internal competition:

1. Maintain situational awareness (defined as the awareness of other initiatives that may create potential conflicts over priorities and resources that impact the success of the project).
2. Plan communications that are horizontal as well as vertical.
3. Address potential conflicts quickly.

Maintain Situational Awareness

A project manager must pay particular attention to other initiatives going on within the business during the project. Many businesses will suffer from "initiative fatigue" because of the large number of plans in progress at the same time. And they are very often not linked together very well. As a result, people feel overwhelmed by the sheer volume of work and changes they are asked to assume. While program management is not an objective for this chapter or this book, some readers will no doubt see some of my suggestions as a part of program management.

> Program management is defined by the Project Management Institute as a group of related projects managed in a coordinated way to obtain benefits and control not available from managing them individually.

You might well ask, "How can communications help that situation?" In truth, you will not change the situation by communications. However, you can keep your project within people's consciousness by faithfully executing your communications plan, including continually repeating the Case for Change, and making adjustments to the communication plan when other initiatives might start to get in the way of your project's success.

For example, if a Six Sigma project requires training for the shipping department within the organization, the project manager must be aware of any other initiatives that shipping has underway because other initiatives may have training requirements also. Most organizations will not be receptive to taking their key personnel off the job for extended periods of training, regardless of the importance and requirements.

In communicating to stakeholders, you must understand how the initiatives fit together and if there are any potential impacts to the critical path for your project and adjust accordingly. This happens very often when the project resource structure has project team members seconded from the business in a matrix structure. Their operational responsibilities will usually trump the work they are assigned for the project. Also, the best individuals will often be seconded to more than one initiative because they are the best! You will probably have to help them manage their priorities, and the answer cannot always be that your project is priority #1 or you will lose any credibility with the team members.

Horizontal and Vertical Communications

In your communications plan, most project managers think (quite rightly) about vertical communications to stakeholders. That is, individuals in the management ranks above them and those who have a significant stake in the success of the project. However, they do not always consider the horizontal communications required. By horizontal, I am referring to the organization chart and to those managers who might be on the same level of authority as the project manager. You must communicate with them, particularly when they have other initiatives underway that might impact your project. Finally, don't forget diagonal communications to other managers from other departments who might not be directly impacted by the project, as well as vendors who might be interested or impacted by the project deliverables.

In communicating, always keep in mind the relationships of these multiple layers of leadership and management within the business. That will help you populate some of the sensitivities (Chapter 5: Common Elements for All Communications) required for various communications. Also, be sensitive to the boundaries of others' authority so you do not inadvertently communicate in a way that shows you do not understand those boundaries. An example might be to ask a group of managers to implement a certain policy or procedure that is important to your success but is clearly beyond their ability to enforce. A mistake like that will cause them to discount any information they receive from you from that point forward. They will be left with the impression, quite rightly, that you don't understand their situation.

> The key point to bear in mind about (political) influence is that it is often an informal method of power and control. Project managers who use influence well in furthering the goals of their projects usually work behind the scenes, negotiating, cutting deals, or collecting or offering IOUs.
>
> *Jeffery K. Pinto*[1]

Address Potential Conflicts Quickly

When potential conflicts arise, do not ignore them in the hope they will go away. Address them as quickly as possible after you have assessed:

- Responsibility
- Authority
- Political climate

---

[1]Jeffery K Pinto, *Power, Politics, and Project Management* (Newtown Square, PA: Project Management Institute, 1998), p. 260.

Responsibility

You will need to be very clear about who is responsible for the situation and begin the exchange of ideas. This is the person you will need to work with to resolve the situation (hopefully). Look for the minimum requirements you have for the situation and be prepared to negotiate within those conditions should the need arise.

Authority

In some situations, you will not be able to successfully negotiate a solution, and you will need to determine who has the authority to make a decision that both you and the other party can live with after it is made.

Political Climate

When you are communicating, always consider the political situation before you act. Keep in mind that whether the message is written on paper or as part of an email, it will tend to be seen by others for a variety of reasons. Always keep in mind those "secondary readers."

How would they receive the information and react to it? And remember for situations of a political nature, keep those messages brief and to the point. Be careful and make each message count. If you are ever in doubt about the wisdom of a written note, then do not send it! Better to call someone on the telephone or meet in person.

> Secondary readers are people for whom the message was not intended (the primary reader), but who have come into possession of that note and might have a strong response to its content.

Project Renewal

Rod Thompson had a difficult situation that reflects the dilemma most project managers face. During the course of the regular

Thursday afternoon Working Committee meeting, Rod learned about a potential conflict with a sales initiative. Gary Stiles, the sales manager on the Working Committee, told the Committee there was concern within the sales department about the amount of time the sales representatives would be required to spend preparing for the CRM system. Rod was aware of a sales initiative related to sales, but he did not see how it could impact his project. He now learned the answer. Research and development had developed a new product line that would be going into production very soon. There were big expectations for the sales team to deliver orders for the new products. The training would take two days of intense work by the sales team to understand the features of the products and the potential target market for them. They were expected to leave the training with a draft plan and revised sales targets for the remainder of the year.

Steve Benson, Rod's training specialist, had already estimated it would take three days of training to properly prepare the sales team to use the CRM system effectively. Taken together with the new product workshops, the sales representatives would be "off the street" for a week! And for the sales team, this was significant since they were paid on commission, and they made no money when they were in training. Plus they would now have additional sales quotas and less time to spend on reaching them. A real revolution was brewing within the sales team, and Rod knew it.

After he had time to think through the situation, he requested a meeting with Paula Dahlberg, his champion, to consider what to do. This could be a highly charged political situation because the leader of the sales team, Nick Winters, was very politically connected with the CEO. However, the risk of not getting the sales representatives trained properly was enormous.

After discussing the situation with Paula, Rod requested that Steve meet with the training people who were preparing the content and timing of the product training. Rod asked Steve to find out when the training was potentially scheduled. He also wanted Steve to determine if there was any way they could combine the CRM training with the product training to save time and still get everyone trained properly on both projects.

In the meantime, Rod and Paula had a meeting with Lise Ramsay, the sponsor, to brief her on the situation. They explained the options they were exploring and said they would come back to her if they needed help. The risks that Rod outlined were primarily associated with the schedule and the associated costs incurred if the schedule slipped. Rod was careful to explain to Lise that the project team was well aware of the importance of keeping the sales team focused, since they are at the front end of the value chain. However, the risks in not having the sales representatives properly trained could lead to the old problem of "garbage in, garbage out" relative to the CRM system.

After considerable work, Steve Benson returned with good news. He and the product rollout team had determined a way to combine the training into the week the sales team had devoted to an offsite meeting that was already scheduled. The only problem was they had not cleared this idea with Nick Winters and without his approval, it would be a non-starter.

> Most successful business people have a keen sense of what is appropriate when talking to others, but many fail to apply this judgment to their writing. Often their writing is far too stiff and formal or too relaxed and colloquial. For an appropriate tone, you need to monitor two attributes of your writing—the degree of motivation required and level of formality.
>
> *Richard Bierck*[2]

---

[2] Richard Bierck, *Find the Right Tone for Your Business Writing: Written Communications That Influence and Inform* (Cambridge, MA: Harvard Business School Press, 2006), p. 86.

Rod then sent an email to Lise since he knew she was out of the office for several days on travel. It read:

To: Lise Ramsay

CC: Paula Dahlberg

Subject: Potential Training Conflict for Sales Reps

Lise,

We have a potential solution to the training conflict we alerted you to earlier, but we will need Nick Winter's approval. It involves using the week of the offsite sales meeting and would require Nick to change his agenda. I would like to discuss the situation in more detail with you and Paula. Please let me know when you are available to talk by phone and we can plan the approach to Nick.

Regards,

Rod Thompson

Notice how clear but concise Rod was in the email. It starts with a positive tone and lets Lise know immediately what it would take to solve the problem—and motivates her to take the recommended action. It was also worded in such a way (the right level of formality) that a secondary reader (for example, in sales) would not be upset or concerned, since it clearly followed the lines of authority within MedTech.

Using the approach to presentations established in Chapter 13: Presenting to Stakeholders During Project Execution, Rod, Paula, and Lise used a draft presentation prepared by Anne Garcia with the help of Gary Stiles, the Working Committee member from the sales department. They worked to refine it for a discussion with Nick Winters. Then they decided how they would present the option and how it might work into Nick's offsite agenda. They then had a brainstorm session about the questions Nick might have and any objections he might raise along with a strategy for answering them. After some discussion about the pros and cons of having Rod or Paula (or both) attend the meeting with Lise, it was decided that

Rod would attend since he would probably be the best one to answer the detailed questions they had outlined during the brainstorming session.

Based on thorough preparation, they received the approval from Nick Winters to use part of his weekly offsite for the CRM training. His only provision was the ability to approve the final agenda after the adjustments required to include the CRM training. Lise was happy to oblige: Another crisis to the schedule averted.

Key Points to Remember

- Recognize that your project is not the only initiative going on in the company and you will need to monitor others for impact on your project.
- Plan for horizontal, as well as vertical, communications to manage competition from other initiatives.
- Handle conflicts quickly and use your champion and communications to manage those conflicts.

If you will follow these guidelines, and keep an eye on other projects vying for attention, you will keep your project front and center with management, and you will receive the support you need to be successful.

Chapter 20

Writing the Close-Out Report

A s Rod Thompson began to organize the close-out report for
the project, he remembered a PMI[1] local chapter meeting he attended where the speaker focused on writing effective close-out
reports. The speaker pointed out that most standard close-out reports are a boring description of statistics related to the project
such as:

- Cost report
- Schedule
- Other project data

The speaker talked about the final report as both a history of
the project and a final evaluation of performance by the project
team members. While the final report for a small project may be no

---

[1]See *Project Management Book of Knowledge* (Newton Square, PA:
Project Management Institute, 2003).

more than a two-page memo, the report for a large project may be ten or twenty pages in length. Rod realized his project would fit into the latter category. The speaker reminded the audience to reference the project diary that almost all project managers keep and the usual logs suggested as standard practice within project management by the Project Management Institute. With all of this data readily available, the speaker contended, producing the final report should be relatively easy.

The speaker proposed instead that the close-out report be viewed as almost a marketing document on the goals of the project and the achievements accomplished by the project team. It should be a narrative of the project that can be read by business leaders to determine how successful the project was from a business perspective.

The speaker suggested that project managers keep in mind that in writing a project close-out report, there are usually two distinct audiences for the report.

1. Business stakeholders who are concerned with the business benefits and who had the problem or issue the project addressed in the first place.
2. Project managers, whether they sit in a project office, program office, or are colleagues who want to understand some of the details surrounding the project.

Before starting to draft the project close-out report, Rod went back to the common elements for all communications he learned from Anne Garcia, his communications specialist, at the beginning of the project (see Chapter 5: Common Elements for All Communications). As he reviewed the common elements, he realized he only really needed to pay attention to three elements for the close-out report: the stakeholder analysis, the purpose, and the strategy for developing the information. All the other elements did not really apply to his report, although he could see some of them applying in a situation that was different from his. He started with the stakeholder analysis and realized he had two groups to address with his close-out report—business stakeholders and project stakeholders.

> Expecting (stakeholders) to treat you fairly because you are a good person is a little like expecting the bull not to attack you because you are a vegetarian.
>
> *Dennis Wholey—*
> *author and host of*
> This is America
> with Dennis Wholey

Business Stakeholders

Rod realized that the stakeholders on the business side were generally the ones who had a problem to solve using the Customer Relationship Management system. In addition, they had either funded the costs of the project or pushed someone else to pay for it. They are most interested in the business benefits being delivered by Project Renewal. For this group, he decided to use a high-level format with these topics:

- Situation
- Business benefits
- Major accomplishments
- Communications with stakeholders
- Lessons learned for future projects
- Punch list of items left outstanding as the project closes
- Very basic project information

Here's how each of these areas looked in more detail.

Situation

In this section, Rod needed to lay out the situation that existed when Project Renewal was being sanctioned. Since these were business people, he reviewed the key goals the business was trying to achieve with this project and what problems they were trying to solve.

Business Benefits

This portion essentially restated the business benefits Project Renewal was asked to achieve and how Rod believed the project had positioned the business to actually achieve them now that the project was finished. Rod included what many project managers recognize—many business benefits will take time to track and record. However, there were some quick wins that were identified right at the beginning. Rod was anxious to claim those quick wins immediately, such as improved process documentation and improved communications between various functional teams. He was also careful to include the expected benefits against each goal outlined in the Situation section of the report. And he identified those benefits that could be reflected in quantitative benefits (real dollars) and then identified qualitative benefits (for example, making order entry easier or more efficient).

Major Accomplishments

This section was fairly short in Rod's report, but he wanted to emphasize some of the key accomplishments of the project such as meeting the schedule and coming in within the projected budget. Another accomplishment was a simple one: overcoming skeptical user groups. Rod realized it was important to remind the business that Project Renewal had indeed made significant accomplishments. Without the reminder, Rod was afraid they might be overlooked.

Communications with Stakeholders

The rationale for this section of Rod's report was simply to reinforce the significant use of communications as the project progressed. He even included some examples of success in overcoming resistance to changes introduced by the project within the operations group. Rod also worked with Paula Dahlberg, his champion, to write a high-level analysis of the quality of the work performed by the project team on behalf of the key stakeholders and match it against the expectations of those stakeholders. He wanted to enlist Paula's help since he wanted to be able to defend the quality from any nay-sayers, and Paula would provide credibility for those statements.

Rod also included special acknowledgment of business people who had been seconded to the project. He wanted to make sure the business stakeholders knew their contributions were both appreciated and critical to the success of Project Renewal.

Lessons Learned for Future Projects

In documenting the lessons learned during the course of the project, Rod was trying to provide feedback to the stakeholders about what his team had learned during the project and how they might apply those lessons in the future. He also decided to include some lessons the project team learned in dealing with certain stakeholder groups as they were implementing the CRM system.

> There are people who learn, who are open to what happens around them, who listen, who hear the lessons. When they do something stupid, they don't do it again. And when they do something that works a little bit, they do it even better and harder next time. The question to ask is not whether you are a success or failure, but whether you are a learner or a non-learner.
>
> *Benjamin Barber, Distinguished University Professor, University of Maryland*

Punch List

In this section Rod wanted to provide the business leaders and the management team of the operations group with a list of items that are still outstanding as the project concludes. Rod identified some items that were determined to be out of scope for the project team to handle, but tasks that operations must still complete even though the project was officially over. He carefully went over this list in advance with Walter Fisher as the representative of the manufacturing group to make sure Walter did not have any objections to the items Rod included. That way, Walter could be called on to help Rod defend the items if the list became an issue later on.

Basic Project Information

In this section, Rod was just reminding the readers of the report of the basic information surrounding the project such as schedule, budget, and quality requirements of the project. He reviewed an analysis of achievements compared to the business case objectives for the project to illustrate how they had achieved those objectives. He would also provide a high-level financial accounting with an explanation of the few large variances from the budget with an explanation of why they had occurred.

Final Observation

As Rod finished his draft for the business stakeholders, he realized this portion of the report would be shorter than the portion he was preparing for the project stakeholders.

Project Stakeholders

For project stakeholders, Rod recognized this group had an entirely different viewpoint regarding what they wanted from the project report. In this portion of the close-out report, Rod would cover all the topics included in the business report, only the level, and type, of detail would change. In each section of a final report for a project, Rod tried to illustrate an

- Analysis of the procedures used in the project.
- Acknowledgment of things that worked and explanation for things that didn't work.
- Recommendations for improvements in future implementations of the project methodology.

He decided to organize the information in the project stakeholder section like this:

- Detailed summary of the project (primarily schedule and budget), including the number of revisions to the original project plan.
- Summary of the business case for the project and how the team had accomplished those benefits.
- Summary of major accomplishments.
- Summary of performance issues, conflicts, and resolutions from the issues log, the risk log, and the change control log.
- Results of each phase of the project, including actual versus forecast dates and the budget versus actual expenses (budget use, additions, and so on, require thorough documentation).
- Total number of approved changes to the scope of the project and the impact of those changes to the accomplishment of the business case as well as the schedule and budget.
- Description of a punch list of items related to transitioning the project to operations that will require further work after the project has been completed.
- Recommendations for changes to future projects (Rod focused on enterprise-wide software projects) so they will run more smoothly and be more compatible with the business.
- An in-depth analysis of reporting procedures and recommendations for improvements.
- An analysis of the project management process as a whole.
- Team's performance (he decided to keep a portion of this section confidential since he recognized that he wanted to identify specific individuals and their performance).
- Special acknowledgments to team members.
- Scheduled date for the after-implementation review.

Expectations of Stakeholders

The rationale for highlighting this section of Rod's report for the project managers was simply to reinforce the significant use of communications to manage stakeholders as the project progressed. He wrote about how successful Project Renewal was in overcoming resistance to changes introduced by the project within the sales and manufacturing groups in particular.

Rod wanted to have input from all core team members since he felt they should either contribute to the report or review its contents for accuracy before it was finalized. As one example, he had Anna Garcia, his communications specialist, write and submit her relevant portions of the final report since he knew she had the correct skills. Then, after editing, and considering the comments of others, he finalized the document.

Packaging the Report

Rod kept all this advice in mind as he chose the framework for the final report. He decided he would break the report into four parts since it would be quite large. Here is the framework for the report:

- Part One: Executive summary. This would be a one- to two-page document summarizing the report's content for key stakeholders who need a quick briefing and do not have time or are unable to digest the entire document (see sample Executive Summary in Figure 20.1).
- Part Two: This part contains information that Rod recognized can be disseminated to all team members, managers, and other interested stakeholders. It includes a detailed review of the project data and an assessment of the project's success in meeting the business case for the project (see details in the next section).
- Part Three: Rod decided this part would address the concerns of the project managers within MedTech. They would be far more interested in some of the detailed mechanics of what the project team did and how they did it to meet their schedule and deliverables. This group would also be looking for lessons learned from Rod's team that could help them complete their projects successfully in the future.

- Part Four: This part was where Rod would include information for management or the executive team *only*. This part had information related to Project Renewal that was confidential in nature. Rod recognized that confidential reports are the most difficult to manage. By making it a separate part of the report, he felt he could control access to this information and manage the security that would be important to MedTech. In working on this part of the report, Rod talked with Paula Dahlberg, the champion, and they agreed to provide the financial reports for the project and highly confidential material and determined the select few people who would be allowed to review this information. Both of them realized this part of the report also contained information that would not be appropriate for team members' eyes; for example, pay rates and/or salaries, team-member performance, and recommendations for future projects.

Executive Summary

Situation

MedTech's legacy system (CTS) did not support the business under current market conditions. The company was finding it more and difficult to respond effectively to customers' orders. CTS made it difficult to schedule the manufacturing process to supply customers with the correct quantities; therefore, the company had to maintain a larger inventory to meet demand. Finally, if MedTech did not replace CTS, the order entry system would have become more and more expensive and difficult to support. The reliability of the system also continued to get worse and caused a lack of efficiency.

Expected Benefits

MedTech will now be able to track the inventory in near real-time. When customers request rush orders, our account representatives should be able to access the inventory and know immediately what products are readily available for shipment. Account representatives will also be able to create "what-if" scenarios prior to entering an order to help the customer maximize discounts and take advantage of promotions.

Our marketing team will be able to easily retrieve customer orders and allow better projections of customer requirements, including new products and services. The CRM will also allow the marketing department to more accurately pinpoint the value drivers within our product lines.

1

The order entry system will be much easier and will

- Remove the need for multiple manual entry points between sales and manufacturing.
- Replace the numerous individual spreadsheets currently used.

Financial Benefits

Based on calculations the following financial benefits are expected:

- Net Present Value (after 5 years) of $39.2 million
- Internal Rate of Return (after 5 years) of 216%

The project team has developed key input and output metrics for all the key stakeholder groups to track benefits and document the benefits as calculated.

Basic Project Information

The project was scheduled for completion at the end of the first quarter of 2008 and was completed on time. The authorized budget was $6 million, and the project came in at $6.3 million with slightly higher costs for licensing when MedTech decided to add some functionality that was not included in the original estimate. As for the quality of the Customer Relationship Management (CRM) system, the help desk is reporting only a slight increase in requests for support vis-à-vis the old system.

2

With this summary, Rod Thompson was able to close out his project and allow all the key stakeholders access to the critical information they needed for the project.

However, his job was not done yet. He still had to communicate with his project team and provide them with feedback on their performance.

Key Points to Remember

- Use the close-out report as a marketing document about the achievements of the project and the project team.
- Determine which common elements for communications are appropriate as you plan to write the report.
- Keep in mind that there are at least two sets of readers—business stakeholders and project stakeholders. Each group will want different information and detail.
- Consider the best way to package the report to convey information and maintain the appropriate level of security.
- Always develop an executive summary when the report is of substantial length.

Chapter 21

Providing Feedback to Your Project Team

One of the final pieces of communication for any project manager is to sit down with the project team members as they are either moving back to their "day job" or leaving altogether if they are contractors. This form of communication may be limited to core team members or may apply to all team members and even outside vendors, consultants, and suppliers. This very special communication should happen in a one-on-one meeting and should cover the performance of the team members.

Since Rod Thompson had people involved in Project Renewal that came to him from other departments or functional groups, the practice within MedTech called upon him to provide an evaluation of the performance of each of those people to his or her direct supervisor. Rod was well aware that within MedTech the evaluations could be used for anything ranging from promotions to new assignments or even layoffs.

He had learned that during a project like Project Renewal, people would be rolling off the project at different times. He knew that he would have to make time to review each team member's contribution before the project terminated and hold a review as the team member departed rather than waiting for project closure. Why? Because he recognized that on a really large project like this one, the time between an individual rolling off the project and the actual time for the review may be a considerable amount of time. He realized from experience that it might be hard to remember exactly what points he wanted to emphasize if too much time had passed before he got around to it. He was also concerned that an individual might not benefit very much personally if the gap between his or her departure and the meeting with Rod was too great.

Another tip Rod had learned over the years in communicating the quality of work to team members was to use concrete examples to illustrate the points he was trying to make. For example, he would say to a team member, "The financial model you built for marketing has been very useful in the analysis of data" versus "The marketing guys really liked the work you did." He had learned the hard way that vague generalities will not have the desired effect of

Involving Others in the Process

In corporations, some companies have standard evaluation procedures that must be followed, and the people from the human resources (HR) department may also insert themselves into the evaluation process. If that situation occurs, chances are HR will provide standard evaluation forms for both you and the employee to fill out. In a situation where team members worked extensively with managers from other stakeholder groups, you might ask managers who worked with those team members to make a contribution to the written evaluations as well. I would not recommend asking individuals who are not managers for their input. Often they are unfamiliar with the process and may create political problems for you later on with insensitive remarks or comments that might be construed as a personal attack.

helping his team members grow in their professional careers and/or become even more valuable as team members on future projects. They needed to know *specifically* what they did well and what they need to do differently to improve.

Finally, during an evaluation, Rod remembered from his own experience to provide both positive and negative feedback to people as he was talking to them. Too often in the past, he had seen project managers focus on areas where people need to improve without mentioning the many things they did correctly or even quite well. (If they didn't do many things well, they would have been fired!)

Here are the basic criteria Rod decided to use for appraising each team member's performance:

- Quality of work
- Timeliness and consistency in meeting deadlines
- Creativity
- Administrative performance
- Ability to work as part of a team
- Attitude
- Communication skills
- Technical ability
- Cost consciousness
- Recommendations for improvement
- Developing a matrix
- Celebrate

Quality of Work

Rod knew the classic definition of quality from the Project Management Institute's *Project Management Body of Knowledge* (PMBOK), which defines quality as "the degree to which a set of inherent characteristics fulfill requirements." He also realized there were a whole host of definitions regarding quality, and people sometimes used different terms when communicating to someone who worked on a project. Rod believed that a more pragmatic approach would be more helpful. In determining the quality of the work produced by a team member, he decided to base his assessment on the answer to these three questions:

1. How many times did someone else have to correct or complete the tasks given to this team member? The frequency of these situations requiring rework was a judgment call, but obviously it was an important consideration.
2. How useful was the work produced by this individual to others as they worked to complete the project? While this may seem the similar to criterion number one, it was not. Rod had seen a consultant, on an earlier project, produce a large volume of work that did not require rework because the output was useless and was simply filed away.
3. Finally, how valuable was the work produced by this team member to him as the project manager and to the stakeholders of the project? Again, this is a subjective matter, but clearly some members of the project are responsible for critical work that was also usually very difficult. Rod decided he needed to take that into consideration when judging the quality of the output of work.

All of these questions helped guide Rod to an informed and clear judgment about the quality of work produced by the various team members. He also used these questions as a basis for discussing his evaluation with the team members.

Timeliness and Consistency in Meeting Deadlines

In this area, Rod focused on the individual's ability to work to the schedule. He felt this was a critical feedback area for project team members. He wanted to be able to give them his feedback, as well as feedback from their team leads, on how timely and consistent

Just remember that timeliness can have different meanings for different people. I remember a project when a key stakeholder complained that the team was not timely in response to his questions. Many of the team members took that to mean they should respond as soon as they had the answer. Others took the attitude that his questions fell into their personal priorities, and they would respond as quickly as they could within the constraints of those priorities. The key stakeholder, however, had a definition that a timely response meant some sort of call or email by the close of business that day—even if the answer might come later! I am convinced that nearly everyone on the project team (myself included) sought to be responsive, but we had a different definition than this particular stakeholder. The lesson learned here for me was to clearly define and communicate to my project what I meant when I told them I needed something in a timely fashion.

these team members were in meeting deadlines. Rod was operating on the assumption that most tasks during a project have dependencies linked to them, and the most valuable team members are those who work to meet those schedules. And they usually told him when they could not meet the schedule and gave a reasonable explanation for missing any deliverable deadlines.

Creativity

Rod recognized that not all project roles need to be creative. He decided that since an evaluation in this area may not be appropriate for all team members, he would identify those for whom creativity was important. He believed that most projects require people to be creative in coming up with solutions to the myriad of problems that occur during a project. Recognizing that fact and communicating it during a project review can be very important to members of the project team in his opinion. He tried to capture examples of creativity by different team members in his project diary so he could refer to them later on as he completed these reviews.

Administrative Performance

This portion of the review pertains to those elements that all project managers usually do not care for but must be done such as time sheets, project updates, and all the myriad details of an administrative nature. While most people are not keen to complete these duties, they are nonetheless critical to the project, and Rod believed he needed to communicate that criticality as part of a project review. For those who were regularly punctual and consistent in handling these items, he felt it was important that he, as the project manager, acknowledge that contribution. Too many project managers he had seen in the past took this effort for granted with an attitude of "that's their job." However, he knew how difficult and time consuming it could be when a project manager or administrator had to constantly chase people to complete these administrative tasks.

Ability to Work as Part of a Team

Teamwork is at the true core of a successful project. Most project managers Rod had talked to over the years believe the old adage that "two heads are better than one." However, that can only happen when members of the project work together as part of a team.

Rod's experience taught him that if he had two candidates to choose from to fill a slot on his project team and one was very smart and talented but behaved like a prima donna, that person would require coddling and work poorly with others on the team. If he had another candidate with less ability or experience but a reputation of working effectively with other members of the team,

A 2003 national representative survey, HOW-FAIR (part of the Level Playing Field Institute at the U.S. Department of Commerce), revealed that Americans think that "being a team player" was the most important factor in getting ahead in the workplace. This was ranked higher than several factors, including "merit and performance," leadership skills," "intelligence," "making money for the organization," and "long hours."

From Wikipedia

he chose the second candidate every time. It was not worth the effort to keep the prima donna, regardless of how talented he or she was. Therefore, Rod strongly believed that the willingness of team members to collaborate should be communicated as part of every project review.

Attitude

Rod had a quote on the wall of his office that accurately summarized his view about attitude. It is from Charles Swindoll, and it reads:

> Attitude is more important than the past, than education, than money, than circumstances, than what other people think or say or do. It is more important than appearance, giftedness or skills. It will make or break a company, a church or a home.

He believed that to be absolutely true and therefore he always spent a portion of the project review session with team members discussing their attitude. Rod was careful to make sure the team members realized he was not evaluating them as a person or communicating to them about their beliefs or values, but only about their attitude toward work, people, and the choices they make every day about how they will behave as part of a project team.

Communication Skills

Rod believed that communication skills in team members was one of the most important skills a person can possess. (Remember back to Introduction of this book, I told you about a global survey we did that showed the number one predictor of success in a project was the communications between the project team and the key stakeholders and among the project team members.) Therefore, he felt it was very appropriate to cover communication skills as part of the evaluation of all team members. He also considered that communications encompassed a broad spectrum, including writing, presentations, and simply speaking clearly and articulately. He hoped to use this discussion as a point for coaching team members for future projects. He believed it would certainly serve them well in the future if he took the time to discuss it thoroughly.

Technical Ability

This portion of the evaluation concerned a team member's work that most people would think of immediately. Since this book is primarily focused on communications, I will not spend too much time in this area. However, one tip I would give you is to go back to Chapter 5: Common Elements of All Communication and review the section on sensitivities. You may also want to review Chapter 12: Using Communications to Handle Risks and look at the information on how to frame this type of discussion. If you keep various sensitivities in mind and frame the situation properly, even if you are going to be critical, you may not upset the team member. If you do not frame the discussion properly, you will likely provoke an explosive situation because most people will become quite defensive if your approach feels to them like a personal attack.

Cost Consciousness

Rod recognized that this issue is another that may not be appropriate for everyone. However, for those on his team who had a responsibility for managing a budget, he believed this was an appropriate communication to have. He believed this same discussion would be appropriate for members of his project team who had responsibility for managing vendors. He framed up the questions in his mind as:

1. How well did they manage the budget within their control?
2. Did they have a good grasp of their rate of expending their funds?
3. How well did they estimate the amount of funds required to complete their area of responsibility?

These questions provided a practical approach to help him assess their performance as well as provide him with specific examples to support the assessment he had made. Rod's attitude was to not spend a significant amount on this subject since the results (how close they came to their budget targets) are concrete and most people would be aware of how well they did in this area. However, if an individual's performance was significantly off-track, he would spend more time discussing the performance and coaching him or her to improve in the future.

Recommendations for Improvement

When communicating to project team members, Rod believed it was most appropriate to start with the positive aspects about people's job performance. He wanted to be sure that he communicated how much he appreciated the good work they did during the course of the project. Just like the earlier in the section on feedback related to the quality of the work, Rod wanted to be specific in providing praise. He believed it was important that individuals know *specifically* what they did well in his opinion. They also needed to be congratulated on these areas of their performance. They knew there would be other negative feedback, but starting with the positive helps them to keep the recommendations for improvement in perspective.

In communicating negative feedback, the first thing Rod did was to share that his purpose in providing this type of feedback was a concern he had to make them more successful in the future. He was careful to focus on direct observations with specifics. He used words like "I've noticed...," "I have seen (or heard)...," "I have had reported to me" as ways to begin the discussion. Otherwise, it would look like he was focusing on the person and not the issues or behaviors. He sought to keep the recommendations very specific and associated with either information or issues or both that Rod was sharing with them.

Rod had a self-imposed rule that if something a person did upset him greatly, he would be very careful to keep his emotions in check when he communicated on this topic. In the past, he had found himself getting upset all over again and realized that strong emotions during the discussion could sabotage his best intentions. For that reason, he would carefully script out what he wanted to say and how he would say it—and then stick to the script and not succumb to the temptation to start to ad lib.

Developing a Matrix

Rod decided to use a matrix of each criterion and grade the individuals based on the priority he placed on each one (Figure 21.1).

As you can see from Figure 21.1, he has divided his assessment to total 100 percent so he can weight various areas as more important than others. In the evaluation, which he did not show anyone else, some of the items were intertwined, and he knew he would have to communicate the linkage. For example, Jessie Cooper had a few issues with her work that required rework on the part of others. That in turn, caused some of her work to miss the scheduled

	Quality of Work	Attitude	Ability to Work in a Team	Timeliness	Cost Consciousness	Administrative Performance	Creativity
Value of the Criterion	15	15	20	20	10	10	10
Team Member							
Anne Garcia	15	12	18	15	10	5	10
Paul Ryan	12	10	15	15	10	7	10
Joshua Larsen	14	15	20	15	10	10	7
Luke Johnson	12	10	15	12	8	5	8
Steve Benson	15	15	20	10	10	7	8
Jessie Cooper	10	15	10	7	5	10	7
Marc Newhouse	15	15	15	20	10	10	5

Performance Criteria

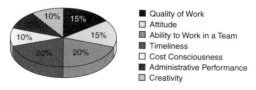

- Quality of Work
- Attitude
- Ability to Work in a Team
- Timeliness
- Cost Consciousness
- Administrative Performance
- Creativity

FIGURE 21.1   Performance criteria.

completion. Therefore, he graded her lower on both quality of work and timeliness. That also impacted his assessment on her working in the team, since he had the impression she did not appreciate the impact she had on her team members when she slipped in quality and timeliness. Using his thoughts about being specific, he was going to provide specific examples for her and coach her on those issues.

For both Paul Ryan and Luke Johnson, his feedback on attitude was their tendency to be negative and complain, which affected their team members. As leaders, he felt they needed to be more cognizant of their influence on the team when they went negative.

Rod liked the tool, even though he knew some could criticize it as subjective, because it forced him to really think about, and evaluate on a scale of one to ten, his team members. In his mind, that more than made up for its shortcomings.

Celebrate

Now that Project Renewal was successfully completed, Rod worked with Paula Dahlberg to plan for a team celebration. They decided to present fun awards to people who performed above and beyond the call of duty. It would mark the official end of the project in everyone's mind.

Paula Dahlberg, the champion, was meeting with Lise Ramsay, the sponsor, to review the celebration plans when Lise announced a surprise. Lise and the leadership team had been very impressed with how well the project team had handled Project Renewal. And the leadership also knew how important the project was to the future of MedTech. So behind the scenes, Lise had been promoting a special celebration for the project team members. At the last leadership team meeting, it had been agreed that MedTech would pay for a weekend in Las Vegas for the entire project team! Paula and Rod were overwhelmed. When they announced what the leadership team was doing for the project team, the response was amazing. They were receiving phone calls and emails by the dozens asking them if this was some sort of April Fool's joke! No one had ever heard of a company's leadership rewarding a project team in this fashion. It made quite a statement about the appreciation of the leadership team for the good work the project team had done. So one last communication to the team came from Lise and Paula to confirm the details—and the broader planning began for the Las Vegas celebration.

Key Points to Remember

- Have the feedback session at the time of a team member's departure and don't wait until later.
- Use concrete examples when explaining your evaluation, whether the point is a compliment or a criticism.
- Provide praise, not just suggestions for improvement.
- Involve other managers and human resources if that is appropriate for your company.
- Determine the criteria that fit each individual and plan what you will say and how you will say it.
- Don't forget to celebrate!

Now you have nearly all the points tidied up and you are ready to cross the finish line.

Chapter 22

Crossing the Finish Line

This final chapter will be devoted to a how to demonstrate the business value you have created and to complete the whole solution to the premise that began the entire book. I will look at the way to establish sustainable changes in the way the people within the operations group work. One of the greatest problems with the deliverables from projects is the lack of sustainability. Once the project team begins to disband and operations is on its own, people begin to fall back into their old habits. I want to stress how to ensure that operations will continue to track the benefits over the long term.

Communicate with the Business on the Value Created

At the end of the project, when the operations group has taken control of the project deliverables, Rod Thompson realized it is time to communicate with the business to explain the benefits it will receive from the new project. He sat down with Paula

Dahlberg, the champion, and Anne Garcia, his communications specialist, to create a communication. Rod wanted to make sure both Paula and Anne understood that in the Close-Out Report, Rod was writing for the senior management team of the company and the key stakeholders. Much of the Close-Out Report highlights the expected Return on Investment for the project. However, that expected ROI will not happen if operations does not use the CRM that the Project Renewal team delivered. That's why Rod is anxious to communicate with the broader organization.

Anne advised Paula and Rod that for the broader audience, the message needed to be centered on the benefits they would personally or collectively receive from the project. To draft the information, the three of them turned again to the Case for Change. It was there the benefits to the people who will use the project deliverables were captured. There was an additional motive in communicating to the broader audience—to remind them of how successfully the implementation went because they participated in the work of the project through their Working Committee and their Change Leaders. Anne felt this communication was a way to congratulate the company for its contributions—with an eye to receive that type of cooperation the next time they were asked to manage a project.

Rod, Paula, and Anne decided to draft two communications and space them out by a week. The first was the congratulatory message to the team and the company for successfully implementing Project Renewal. The second message would be to circulate the new performance measures for operations that come out of the project team's work. The target for this audience would be the managers within MedTech who would find some of these new measures on their performance contract and needed to understand them a little better.

Performance Measures in Operations

The next key to making the results of the project sustainable over time would be to remind the business people that now that the project is finished, it is their turn to take those project deliverables and use them correctly to deliver the return on the investment made by the company.

The first part of message the managers would be to explain the need for quantifiable measures help to justify the investment made by MedTech in buying and implementing the CRM. Only by tracking measures to results can a real justification occur.

The message would explain the two types of measures—output and input.

- Output measures: The process metrics results to monitor the value generated. For the CRM, examples of the output measures would include growth in sales to existing customers and customer satisfaction and growth in the number of new customers from within the prospect group.
- Input measures: Process metrics to monitor the use of the process such as a decline in the inventory stored, reduced cycle time from contract to delivery, and others.

For the message around performance measures, Rod wanted them to also appreciate that measures can also provide comparative benchmarks against some of MedTech's competitors as well as an early warning signal of suboptimal performance. Input and output comparisons will act as pointers to improve performance by working to improve the processes across MedTech. An important point in the communications around metrics was the involvement of the Working Committee. Rod and his business lead, Paul Ryan, worked with various members of the Working Committee to establish the correct measures for MedTech.

In choosing measures he and the Working Committee communicated to managers, Rod wanted to be sure they included those measures (dollars, time, number of errors) carefully to give these managers real insights into how the project deliverables are really working once they go into day-to-day operations. Paula Dahlberg pointed out that the project team would also need to clarify the assumptions made in recommending those measures, since the managers would probably question them unless they knew the assumptions the project team and the Working Committee used.

Finally, Lise Ramsay, the sponsor, was very keen to make sure that the managers understood they were clearly accountable for collecting and reporting on the measures in the eyes of the senior leadership team. Lise was of the opinion that if no one clearly responsible, no one will sign up for doing this work after the fact.

Communicate with All Team Personnel

Rod began to instruct all team personnel in writing as to when the project would end. This put pressure on the stragglers who needed a little more time to complete their tasks. Rod had a suspicion that more time was needed for some people, so he set the end date several weeks into the future and started giving then weekly reminders of the drop-dead date. For real problem people, he began to visit them daily to assess their progress and remind them of the date.

Rod also asked Paul Ryan, his lead business analyst, and Josh Larsen, his technical team lead, to notify all outside suppliers and vendors that the project would completely close down in the coming weeks. Since the project is ending, he wanted them to get the message that Rod and MedTech would not accept bills from any of those vendors received 30 days after the close-out date. (Rod realized, of course, that he would have to be flexible on this one. However, he also realized it is really a tactic to get the bills coming in the door from vendors as quickly as possible.) It also saves Rod and MedTech some interest charges, and really prompt payment may knock a percentage off the total project bill. He asked Marc Newhouse to check purchase orders to see what was still outstanding and report back to him.

Rod also asked his team leads to inform managers of temporary employment agencies and contractors, in writing, that the project's termination date was near. He hoped this would provide the managers in those companies

> Success has a thousand fathers, but failure is an orphan.

time to find other opportunities for these people or to move them back into their usual job responsibilities.

The After-Implementation Review

A common practice among experienced project managers, particularly on large projects, is to conduct an after-implementation review. Rod reviewed his reference books on how to conduct an after-implementation review as one way to ensure that operations continues to use the project deliverables correctly and in a sustained way.

Rod noted that an after-implementation review meeting is usually scheduled between three to six months after the project is closed out, with the key team members and some of the stakeholders. The review is a discussion about what has happened since the project was turned over to operations. Because of other commitments and initiatives on the horizon, Rod decided to conduct his session about ten weeks after the project closed.

In reviewing his reference materials, Rod recognized the value in getting a little distance from the project to help everyone gain some insights on what went well and what they would do differently in the future. Also he realized that any problems or surprises that are likely to occur will happen in those first few months. That information would be very helpful in crafting the lessons learned.

> If you need information from some people who may not be available for the after-implementation review, interview them before they leave so you have their input for the meeting.

Finally, Rod worked with Paula on a briefing to the operations management team. They were very keen to communicate the value delivered by Project Renewal. He also want to brief the executive team, so he and Paula included Lise in the preparation. All of them felt the importance of this presentation was to set the correct expectations within management about the sustainability of the rewards from the project (refer to Chapter 13: Presenting to Project Stakeholders During Project Execution). The assumption they operated under was if the management team expected the project deliverables (namely the CRM and the associated business processes) to be used, they are much more likely to be used and used correctly.

In Conclusion

Throughout the book, the emphasis has been on the importance of communications in a successful project. Remember back to the beginning and those global project managers who said the best predictor of a successful project was how well the project team communicated with their stakeholders and among themselves.

There are common elements for any type of communication, and they should be either applied or considered, whether the message is written or oral. If you will follow those principles faithfully, they will never let you down.

All the way through the book, I have tried to demonstrate that conveying information to your stakeholders is vitally important in

- Managing their expectations.
- Keeping leadership engaged and supportive.
- Handling risks to prevent or control issues.
- Preparing operations for your project deliverables.

And always prepare your communication plan with as much care and thought as you do your Work Breakdown Structure and your schedule. It will pay dividends from the beginning.

Finally, one last piece of advice—always target any communication to a distinct audience with a specific purpose in mind. Do that, and you will be considered a genius among your peers and your customers!

Index

About the Author

G. MICHAEL CAMPBELL, PMP
PRESIDENT, MCA, International LLC.

Mike Campbell is the President of MCA and has over 25 years experience in working with Fortune 500 companies, including numerous energy sector companies such as BP, Chevron, Shell, Schlumberger, Baker Hughes, and Occidental Petroleum, as well as smaller companies and nonprofit organizations such as the American Cancer Society. Mike works with companies who want to increase their success rates with implementation of technology, strategy, and process redesign projects.

He is an internationally recognized expert with four books on project management and communications. Mike has been a featured speaker at a number of global conferences sponsored by groups such as the Society of Petroleum Engineers and the International Quality and Productivity Center. He has published several articles in publications such as the *Journal of Petroleum Technology*, *Hart's Energy*, and the *American Oil and Gas Journal*. He has also been an adjunct professor at York University, Toronto, Canada, and the University of Houston, Houston, Texas, USA.

Mike has a Bachelor's degree from Ohio University, a Master's degree from John Carroll University and has earned the title of Project Management Professional from the Project Management Institute. He is also Certified in the Governance of IT (CGEIT) by ISACA and ITGI.